10/21/81

To Chuck

Long Time Associate

As they We Grow

Each

Dave Pons

G.67.

When the Going Gets TOUGH

When the Going Gets TOUGH

Billy Burden

Fleming H. Revell Company
Old Tappan, New Jersey

Scripture quotations are from the King James Version of the Bible.
"As a Man Thinketh" by Billy Burden, Copyright © 1962 by Billy Burden. Used by permission.

Library of Congress Cataloging in Publication Data
Burden, Billy, date
   When the going gets tough.

   CONTENTS: When the going gets tough.—From charred legs to the world's fastest mile: Glenn Cunningham.—Turning scars into stars: Art Linkletter.—"God, I dedicate my entire day to you": Marguerite Piazza. [etc.]
   1. Conduct of life—Case studies. I. Title.
BJ1581.2.B785   248.4   80-15731
ISBN 0-8007-1138-6

TO Dad

This book is dedicated to a man who stayed so tough for so long—my Dad.

Many who knew Dad and observed him in and out of the hospital have said to me, "Your dad sure is tough." Others have said, "Your dad is a fine example for others who are having it tough." Some have asked, "How is he able, with all of his problems, to stay so tough?"

Dad had some answers a lot of people simply do not have.

Seeing him stay tough day in and day out, day after day, many days near death, gave me the inspiration and the dedication to write this book.

For myself, and for others who are having it tough, I say, "Thank you, Dad."

Contents

Billy Burden and Dr. Norman Vincent Peale

Foreword

When the Going Gets Tough, by Billy Burden, is just the kind of book that is needed by everyone of us. For haven't we all had times, indeed may be having them right now, when the going is tough? How to handle oneself under such difficult circumstances is very important knowledge.

In this book Mr. Burden fascinatingly tells the stories of persons who overcame tremendous obstacles and how they did it. I am certain that every reader will find, among these narratives of strong, overcoming people, one or more with whom he can personally identify and so learn to handle his own problems victoriously.

The human stories in this highly inspirational book are from some who are unknown to the general public, and others are about persons whose names are known everywhere.

I have shared the platform on speaking engagements many times with Billy Burden and therefore am aware of his outstanding ability to move and inspire people. He is, himself, an enthusiastic believer in human potential and is a reliable guide in how to meet problems, stand up to them, and overcome them.

Billy Burden is an attractive personality, and his strong faith comes through on the platform, in one-to-one meetings and in the pages of this book.

When the Going Gets Tough is a book that will give you fresh courage, wise insights, and a restored faith in your own ability to overcome any problem.

Norman Vincent Peale

Acknowledgments

I suppose every author has certain people to whom he or she feels grateful for their assistance and for their encouragement.

Certainly, I feel a special appreciation to those featured in this book who have shared and even bared their lives to me, so that together we might be able to help others.

Too, I am especially grateful to four very special people who helped to make this book possible.

JEFF KLINE

A young man dedicated to his family and to his work, Jeff Kline is a feature writer with the *Lakeland Ledger,* an affiliate of the New York Times Company. He specializes in personality profiles and is an assistant to the feature editor. He not only helped me to compile the material for this book, but he helped me to write every chapter. Jeff has become a real friend.

WESLEY RYALS

The "eagle eye" of an expert brings a feeling of peace and relaxation to an author who isn't quite sure of certain grammatical questions. Wesley Ryals is head of the English Department at Florida Southern College in Lakeland, Florida, and his careful scrutiny of the manuscript was greatly appreciated. He is not only a friend, but he is a Christian friend who shared a dedication to the purpose of this book.

DIANE MAYHER

An efficient and pleasant secretary who never wavered once in the face of my hectic schedule and quick telephone calls, Diane truly got "caught up" in this book as she was typing the manuscript. Her dedication is greatly appreciated.

JOYCE BURDEN

A Christian wife has to be one of the greatest assets any man can have. I thank God every day for helping me find Joyce. She knew my purpose in writing this book, and she has shared each moment of it with me. To Joyce, I quote from Robert Browning, "Grow old along with me! The best is yet to be."

When the Going Gets TOUGH

I
When the Going Gets Tough

WHEN THE GOING GETS TOUGH, the tough get going.

Great!

And most of us have heard that cliché before. But the more important question is—how do the tough get tough when the going gets that way?

And that's what this book is all about!

Most of the time, getting tough is a matter of choice. Once in a while, it is not.

Sometimes we have to get tough if we are going to survive. We have no choice about the matter.

How many times have you heard of someone who was trapped in a burning automobile or an airplane and exerted strength beyond seemingly physical limitations and freed himself from the wreckage? He had to get tough to survive. He had no choice about the matter.

I am reminded of the story my father tells about how he learned to swim. His brother and some of the rural neighbor boys had been trying day after day to teach him in the farm pond. But all to no avail. Finally, in total disgust, they each agreed that they would throw him in over his head and leave. Now, this is not a recommended method of swimming instruction, but, in my father's case, it worked. Dad said that when he came up for air the third time and couldn't see anyone, he decided that it was time to start swimming. In other words, he had to get tough. It was a matter of survival.

Dad's story brings to mind one about the little toad who was caught in a crack in the middle of the highway. All of the other little toads tried desperately to pull him out of the crack, but as night approached, they had failed. They all agreed that it was impossible to get him out of the crack, so each one bid him a final farewell and headed home for a night's sleep. The next morning, knowing that he would be run over and killed during the night, they returned to pick up his remains for burial. But when they hopped over to where they had left him the night before, he was not to be found. Finally, they heard him chirping in the grass along the side of the highway. They went hopping over to inquire about his well-being. They asked him what good fortune had come his way. He said to them, "You remember, last night when you left, I was caught in that crack out there in the pavement. Well, after you left, along came a great big truck, and I had to get out of that crack!"

In cases like this, it is easier to get tough than not because it is a matter of survival. Either one gets tough or else one does not survive. But what about the times when survival is not at stake? These are the times when it is tough to get tough.

What about the person who is seriously injured in an accident and loses the use of his legs? He can resign himself to the fact that he will be confined to a wheelchair the rest of his life, or he can vow to regain mobility in his legs, even if it means learning to walk all over again.

What about the person who has lost a loved one through the act of another? He can live with hate and bitterness the rest of his life, or he can cultivate compassion in his heart and rise above his feelings of revenge.

What about those who are born into this world with physical traits that would act as limitations from birth? They can live in a world of self-pity, or they can rise above their limitations, often turning liabilities into assets.

What about the person who loses his eyesight? He can accept a world of total darkness, never again seeing the beauty around him, or he can learn to see it through the rest of the senses the Lord gave him.

The child from a background of poverty can accept mediocrity the rest of his life, or he can fulfill his fondest dreams for attainment.

The alcoholic can continue to drink himself into a grave of despair and ultimate death, or he can stop drinking—just for today—one day at a time.

The businessman whose business has just "gone under" can give up and accept the fact that he will be an employee the rest of his life, or he can pick up the pieces and start all over again, full of the same expectations that filled him at the start of his initial efforts.

The sinner can continue to ignore the Day of Judgment, or he can set about righting his wrongs and living a life committed to the glory of God.

In each of these cases, it is a personal decision whether or not something constructive is going to be done. Why is it a personal choice? Because immediate survival is not at stake and our instincts do not take over for us. An immediate decision does not have to be made. In fact, a decision does not ever have to be made. The person can accept his situation and remain status quo instead of electing to move beyond the restraints of his circumstances.

But what about those who do want to unshackle themselves from the chains that bind them? How do they get tough?

What is it that enables some men and women and boys and girls to pick themselves up by their own "bootstraps" after being knocked down? How do some keep on picking themselves up when they are repeatedly knocked down time after time? What is it that enables some to be such great self-starters?

How do they keep on keeping on?

How do some, with every possible handicap, go on to achievement after achievement, while others, with every possible opportunity before them, seem to bury themselves in the very mire of mediocrity? What is the difference?

Two very traumatic experiences in my life forced me to find the answer to the question—how do the tough get tough when the going gets that way? As I have traveled around the country teaching my memory seminars, I have met countless individuals who have obviously found the answer to this question too. But I have also encountered hundreds who did not have the foggiest notion that there even existed an answer to this question, let alone finding it.

Through the years, this latter observation has disturbed me greatly.

Wouldn't it be nice if we could hand these people the answer to this question in a beautifully wrapped package? No—and for a very simple reason. When someone gets something for nothing, he places little value on it.

So it is with the answer to the question—how do the tough get tough when the going gets that way?

All of us must, in our own way, not only have a burning desire for the answer to this question, but we must be willing to search for the answer if we are to find it. Otherwise it will elude us like the pot of gold at the end of the rainbow.

But wait—you must be searching for the answer. Otherwise, you wouldn't be reading this book.

Certainly, I have come to the conclusion that there is not a single answer to our question, but there are four closely related answers. And the four answers can easily be summed up in eight little words. Eight little words? Yes, eight little words, which you will discover as you read through the pages of this book just as surely as if they were chiseled on the granite foundation of your life. And because you will be ready for them when you find them, you will quickly recognize them. They will glisten for you like a precious diamond reflecting light, pulling your eyes to their truth and to their beauty.

Not only will you recognize these eight little words, but when you find them, you will know their meaning and understand it.

For many years, my wife, Joyce, and I, through our seminars and through the Positive Thinking Rallies at which I appear, have been able to share these answers with men and women and boys and girls all over America. Our greatest rewards come from receiving letters and phone calls from those whose lives have been helped by the answers.

But those who have been helped were truly in need of the answers, and they were ready for them when they found them.

In the festive parade of life, as the gates of opportunity are slammed in our faces, as passions are calmed, as retirement is mandated upon us, and as a thousand other traumatizing dramas unfold, it is little wonder that we often ask ourselves, "Is it worth the effort?"

Few people would argue with the deduction that we are living in a time of stress and strain. Like a tornado out of the Southwest, the breakdown in our moral fiber is leaving a path of destruction that is taking its toll in our lives. These devastating winds are destroying the very core of our mental and physical well-being—the family.

Divorce is at an all-time high. Economic conditions bring unwelcomed pressures. Crime is on the rampage. Apathy and complacency rage. Everywhere we turn, we can see a world that invites us to give up—to admit defeat.

Today, in the vast arena of life, millions of men and women and, yes, boys and girls, are existing in sheer desperation. Their lives are plagued with panic and worry. They are neurotic, fearful, and frustrated. And their feelings stem from two kinds of failures: past failures and prospective failures. The intensity of the moment strikes them with a numbness resulting in a feebleness that prevents them from exploring their resources for solutions to their problems. This numbness intensifies as they relive past failures and anticipate future ones.

But the real tragedy of life is not in failing; it is failing to attempt. It is not in what we suffer, but in how close we come to happiness without finding it. Too often we are like the prospector who misses, only by inches, the gold that those who come after him will discover.

Everyone who walks on this earth fails at sometime or another in some area of his life. Some allow their defeats to cause them to drop their high ideals. Some bemoan their failures. Others allow their virtues to decay. Others stumble into mediocrity. Still others slip into the slavery of vice. Others experience weariness, a deterioration of health, or economic setbacks. All of these failures sing out together in a mournful chorus: "If only I had my life to live over again."

At the lowest ebb in my life, when I was close to ending it all, I heard an announcer on a radio station say something that helped to sustain me. He simply said, "Some people profit by their experiences, and some never get over them."

Life is just one experience after another, and we must learn to profit from each of our experiences.

The anxieties in our lives relate to the sand passing through the hourglass. Man is the only time-conscious creature. Man alone can recall the accumulation of his past in such a way that it bears heavily on the present moment. Man is also the only creature who can bring the future into the present in such a manner as to imagine it as if it were happening now. And because man can bring the past to the present with his memory, and his future to the present with his imagination, he can also bring unhappiness to his life through excessive dwelling on past failures and an overindulgence in the prospects of future failures.

The heritage of "what has been" can bring on despair, pessimism, and complacency. The prospects of "what might be" can bring on fears, anxieties, and worries.

Today, psychiatry probes and ponders these two areas in an effort to find concrete answers to the problems that plague troubled lives.

How, then, is a proper balance reached, and what is it that enables the tough to get tough when the "chips are down"?

Eight little words? Yes, eight little words.

First of all, we must be willing to accept God's plan for our lives. We must accept His standard. If we try to move through the drama of life with self-made standards, we will be saddened, and our lives will be empty. We must be willing to come up to God's standard, and we must realize that He does have a plan for each of our lives.

Our watch can be neither fast nor slow if it is the only measure of time in the world. Only if there is another timepiece against which we can check our watch can we establish its accuracy.

By the same token, we cannot accurately measure ourselves

merely against ourselves. We have to have a standard against which we must check ourselves, and that standard must not be shallow where character and self-discipline are concerned. If we are going to be happy and fulfilled, our standard must be the one established for us by our Creator when He was sculpturing a plan for our lives.

When we accept His plan for our lives, we can rejoice in the fact that His standard does not place limitations on our lives, but in the final analysis, His standard expands our freedoms if we keep our lives in tune.

The more the conductor rehearses the orchestra, the more it must be periodically tuned. So it is with our lives. God loves us too much to allow us to be comfortable with unnecessary weaknesses. God wants the very best from us.

The violinist in the symphony wants the best from his instrument, so he tightens each string until it is capable of producing a perfect sound. If the string could, it would probably protest loudly the pain it has to endure in order to come up to standard pitch. We tune our pianos to a standard pitch of 440-A. So it is with our lives. God has a plan for each of us, and if we are going to be happy and fulfilled, we must tune our lives to God's standard. We must be willing to accept God's plan for our lives.

A child is quick to ask why. He tears up his toys to find out what makes them run. But there are times when we cannot tear ourselves up to find out answers. There are times when we must accept God's purpose for us.

When we do this, we can transform a life of doubt and fear into one of triumph and victory.

Without acceptance, however, fear of the unknown prevails, and this provides a fertile field for anxiety.

But when we accept the fact that, regardless of our circumstances, God does have a purpose for us; when we accept this as fact, the lonely can escape from their imprisonment.

Those who are depressed can find light to dispel their otherwise impenetrable darkness. Those who live with feelings of being unloved and of being rejected can find acceptance and the ability to give and receive love. Those who are tormented by feelings of guilt which seem indelible can wash those feelings away. And when we free ourselves from the tyrannies of repressed memories, we are able to realize that positive thought is more powerful than negative thought because positive thought is in tune with the orchestra of the universe.

But sometimes God allows us to let our lives get so badly out of tune that we cannot, by ourselves, get them back in tune. He does this so that He can perform a miracle for us. This is another one of His ways of showing His love for us. And isn't it comforting to know that when our lives are so badly out of tune, we can turn to God for help? He is always there.

As a youth, Demosthenes not only stuttered but also had a very displeasing voice. He could never have become one of the world's greatest orators if he had not worked to tune the weaknesses in his life to standard pitch. Abraham Lincoln lost several bids for public office before he was elected president of the United States. Beethoven rose above defeat and did not let the fact that he could never hear the music he wrote stop him from writing it. Milton used his blindness as an inspiration for one of his greatest poems. The author of *Gone with the Wind* had the manuscript rejected twenty-four times before it was finally accepted.

When Job was subjected to suffering, he asked God why he was born, and why he had to suffer. Instead of answering Job's questions, God asked Job to answer more important questions. Then Job realized that God's questions were more profound than men's answers.

God's ways are not always our ways, but the salvation of our soul is far more important than the pain of the moment.

My mother used to say, "Everything happens for the best."

If I heard her say that once while I was growing up, I heard her say it a thousand times. And now I understand its truth.

Divine wisdom can bring good from bad if we will accept God's plan for our lives.

We would not think of leaving the theater during the first act, just because the hero was shot. The dramatist has prepared a plot. Nor should we walk out during the first act of God's plan for our lives. It is the last act in the drama of life that brings with it God's applause and our crown of victory.

The things that occur in our lives are not always intellectually understandable, but they are always acceptable if we have faith in God's plan. And when we accept God's plan for our lives, we are touching a bit of Eternity.

A chisel in the hands of Michelangelo could produce a better statue than the same chisel in the hands of a novice. So it is with our lives. We become fulfilled when we accept God's plan for our lives.

The pursuit of our dreams under our own power may keep us busy, but in the end, if they are not God's dreams, they come to nothing.

The phrase that sanctifies our lives is "Thy will be done."

If our lives ended here, the closing of gates, the deterioration and passing of the years, indeed, our very existence would often become unbearable. But the turbulent waves of the surface leave the depths of the ocean totally undisturbed.

We must be willing to look beyond the surface to the inner depths of our soul.

We must heed the command Socrates made when he said, "Know thyself!"

This business of knowing ourselves is paramount in being able to be tough when the need arises. The turning point in any life comes when that person begins to understand the person in the mirror.

Don't ponder so long about what you think, but ponder long and hard about why you think it.

Eight little words? Yes, eight little words.

In all of the universe, man is the only creature who can probe the inner depths of his mind and study the reflections of his inner being to determine what he should do. A rock, a flower, a bird, a rabbit—these things cannot search out their thoughts to label them. Only the human spirit can be both the subject and the object of a thought. Man can admire himself, be angry with himself, or even condemn himself. Man's ability to look at himself in the mirror makes him the most superior creature in the universe, but it also makes him susceptible to mental and physical disorders if he is unwilling to make an unprejudiced examination of himself and his acts.

We are all conscious beings, but too many of us are not conscious of what makes us "tick." We don't know our real selves. Too often we are afraid to take a real look at ourselves.

The pressures of the moment often cause us to flee from the pains of self-examination and possible self-understanding. We are afraid of what we might find. Sometimes, in extreme cases of desperation, we are so afraid of what we might find that we seek unconsciousness as a means of escape.

The alcoholic seeks total obliteration of the thing that is causing mental anguish. A cure for alcoholism often necessitates facing the very problem the alcoholic is seeking to escape. Of course, this effort is unsuccessful without self-understanding.

Those interested in the problems of the day cannot help wondering if the rampaging interest in television and movie horror stories is not an affirmation that millions need to solve important problems in their lives; but rather than face the difficult task of piecing together the parts of the puzzle to their troubled lives, they turn instead to the tormented lives of others. They seem to thrill to the bad news in the headlines. The man who has a hell of his own seems to rejoice for the moment when he can escape his hell by transferring his attention to the hell someone else suffers.

At best, to "know thyself" is tough. But self-knowledge is a must if our fiber is going to be tough.

We must judge ourselves by first knowing our purpose. And our purpose should be to find happiness in our lives — the kind of happiness that comes only by reaching for our highest potential.

Self-understanding is the key to most problems that confront us. Self-understanding does away with boredom. It gives us zest. It gives our radar fine tuning.

But when we loiter on the shore of the superficial self, we suffer from a feeling of emptiness because our inner being knows that we are not being honest with ourselves. It knows that we are not reaching out to our potential. But when we gain self-understanding, we do not settle for shallow satisfactions — we reach for the stars. The freeze that paralyzes the actions of our lives is thawed. And when the goals of our lives are established, we learn to become less defensive, less sensitive. The real self inside us becomes a self-respecting, fulfilled self with compassion and love for others.

At the end of each day, the prudent merchant reviews his cash register tapes to examine the debits and credits for the day's business. We should check the debits and credits of our lives. What have we put in? What have we taken out? And as we begin to know ourselves, we learn to count our blessings! Then we are able to say to ourselves, "I can!"

More often than not, we can turn our lemons into lemonade, if we have researched our blessings.

Eight little words? Yes, eight little words.

The ability to coordinate the faculties of one's mind with the instincts and actions of one's body is self-control. But which comes first? Toughness or self-control? Toughness helps to orchestrate one's life and makes the crescendo possible. But toughness is a result of self-control. It is not a matter of which came first, the chicken or the egg. The finest symphony on earth would sound boring and produce no music if each note were played at the same volume level. But the instruments must first be tuned before the conductor worries about the crescendos.

So it is with life. We must establish certain areas of self-control before we can become tough.

Well, what attributes of self-control do we desire? How tough do we need to be?

The person who has been advised by his doctor that he has terminal cancer needs more self-control than the one who has been told that the burning in his stomach is an ulcer — particularly if he wants to live to see his firstborn grandchild or attend his daughter's wedding or even prove his doctor wrong in the number of months he will live.

There can be no question about the fact that the self-control, the self-discipline, you possess determines your toughness.

How much pain are you willing to endure in order to learn to walk again? Are you willing to fall five times each day, or would you be willing to fall ten times? Are you willing to pay the price for success? There are no gains without pains.

Self-control produces faith in oneself and an exit. God never shuts a door but what He opens a window. The nonbeliever has problems finding an exit and therefore has problems finding hope. And it is hope that helps us to act.

Knowing that we can accomplish our goals in life is merely a habit of reaffirmation of the hope that enables us to act.

The tiny drops of water leaking through a dike can soon lead to the total ruin of the dike and to ultimate flooding. So it is with our habits. Good or bad, they eventually lead to a compulsion. If they are bad, if we do not keep them finely tuned, they can lead to self-destruction. If they are good, they can repair, mend, heal, overcome, propel, and sustain.

A tiny strand of thread can easily be broken. But many strands, woven together, become a strong rope.

So it is with mental habits. Good mental habits help to ensure our mental and physical well-being. Bad ones bring on sickness and despair. And good or bad, our habits become "second nature" to us and control our lives.

Deep within the depths of our subconscious minds, all of us have certain capabilities and powers at our disposal waiting to be used as we ourselves command. And good habits allow these commands to be heeded with fast response.

Our human minds have two faculties: One is speculative and is directed to knowledge—the belief that we can; the other is the will, which carries our knowledge into action. It is our will which determines our actions.

Hidden deep within our very nature is a storehouse of flammable material which cannot and will not be ignited except by a command from our will.

Damp wood kindles slowly under a fire, but a strong breeze will fan it into flames with black clouds of smoke. Little by little the smoke is dissipated, as the moisture dries up, and the blaze spreads freely over the whole crackling pile till the wood is wholly changed into the likeness of fire. Then the crackling ceases; nothing is to be seen save the victorious fire, glowing in the profound peace of great silence: first, fire and flame and smoke; then the fire and the flames, but smoke no more; last of all, pure fire, with neither flame nor smoke. As is the damp wood, so are our carnal hearts.

There is in each of us this inner being called our will. How plentiful our victories would be if, when the winds of adversity would chap our faces, instead of turning away, we would shout out, "Where there's a will, there's a way!" And it's really true, but the will must spring from the inner being within us. We must nurture this inner being each day if it is going to respond for us when the "chips are down."

We must feed and condition this inner being with a diet of positive thoughts harvested from a garden of firm convictions.

But too often we allow a dry rot to undermine all that could be good in our inner being. Too often, we allow an avalanche of deterioration to be brought on by doubt, fear, and skepticism until our inner and even our whole being is in a state of collapse.

How small a spark it takes to set fire to a vast forest! And that is what the will is, the spark that can light our fire of action.

Eight little words? Yes, eight little words.

Nothing needs to be disciplined more than the will, for it is the will that is the conductor of our lives and tells our bodies what acts to perform. Our intelligence provides us with the target, but it is our will that shoots the arrow.

Eight little words? Yes, eight little words. Eight little words to give us the four answers to our question.

In the art gallery, we marvel at the works of the great masters. In the gallery of life, every conceivable existence is put on display.

The lives which are unveiled on the pages which follow were carefully chosen. While all of these lives are uniquely different, in one respect they are very much the same. Each was able to get tough when the going got that way.

I know you will find inspiration from these lives and, as you study them closely, you will find the answers to our question.

Glenn
Cunningham

2
From Charred Legs to the World's Fastest Mile

GLENN CUNNINGHAM is truly a legend in his time. His triumphant story has no doubt been told by more speakers than any other story of modern day victory.

To have grown up in Kansas when I did and not to have known about the great runner Glenn Cunningham would have been unthinkable. As a matter of fact, about the only way a person growing up in Kansas back then could not have known about Glenn Cunningham would have been to live completely incommunicado from fellow Kansans.

The superintendent of schools in my district had been in the school system where Glenn attended when Glenn was in grade school. This teacher used to motivate me and encourage me by telling me stories about the great miler, Glenn Cunningham.

Glenn was one of the greatest runners this country has ever produced. During the 1930's, the "Iron Man of Kansas," as he was called, was America's most durable middle distance runner.

He was a half-mile and mile specialist. His record for the world's fastest mile, set during the AAU championships in March, 1934, stood for nine years before being broken. He set new records in the half mile and mile and in the 800 and 1,500 meter races. He represented America in the 1932 and 1936 Olympics, winning the silver medal in the 1,500 meter in 1936.

And when one ran the mile on his high-school track team, as I did, Glenn Cunningham was the man he tried to emulate. Glenn was a hero of mine long before I had the chance to meet him over two decades later in Omaha, Nebraska.

Today, I consider myself fortunate in being able to call him my friend. I have had the privilege of appearing on numerous programs and seminars with him.

Yet, Glenn is more than a friend and a hero. He is the embodiment of the spirit, the strength, and the desire it takes to overcome adversity and emerge a winner. For Glenn Cunningham came within a hairbreadth of dying, and even closer to having his legs amputated.

Glenn, his two brothers, and his sister were the first to arrive at the wooden schoolhouse that cold winter morning in 1916. While their sister stayed outdoors to play on the swing, seven-year-old Glenn and an older brother played tic-tac-toe on the blackboard while Floyd, Glenn's thirteen-year-old brother, went to build a fire in the potbellied stove.

Floyd started to pour what he thought was kerosene into the stove to light the fire and get it going. Although the boys did not know it, the school had been used the previous evening for a meeting by a local organization. Gasoline had been put in the can and the coals at the bottom of the stove were still red-hot.

The gasoline exploded when it hit the hot coals. Glenn and his brother turned from the blackboard to find the school ablaze.

Within seconds they were standing in the middle of an inferno. Glenn attempted to climb on top of a desk to get his feet and legs out of the flames, but already his clothes were on fire, searing and burning his legs.

Somehow the three boys made it outside, where their sister threw sand on them to smother the flames. Then, in a state of shock, they ran the two miles back home. When they arrived, Glenn's oldest sister was there with the two youngest children. His mother was at his uncle's where she had been caring for Glenn's grandmother who was ill. Glenn's sister took one look at the boys and frantically sent for a doctor, who was eleven miles away and who would take hours to arrive.

The boys were put to bed immediately, but there was precious little that could be done for severe burns back in those days.

Nine days later, Floyd died.

Glenn's legs were so severely burned that the doctor at first thought he too might die. He told Glenn's parents that their son would never walk again. For several days, the doctor even debated whether or not to amputate the charred legs. But finally, after many weeks, the doctor was able to tell Glenn he could get up. He only meant that Glenn could sit up in bed and look out the window, if he wished. Glenn thought the doctor meant that he could get up and go outside and play. He swung himself out of bed and attempted to stand. But he had no feeling or strength in his legs, and he collapsed in a heap beside the bed.

The doctor then sadly told Glenn what he had already told Glenn's parents: Glenn would never walk again.

"I'll walk. I know I will," Glenn cried as they put him back into bed.

Without knowing it, he was already finding the truth of the Scriptures:

> . . . If ye have faith as a grain of mustard seed, ye shall say
> unto this mountain, Remove hence to yonder place; and it
> shall remove; and nothing shall be impossible unto you.

Matthew 17:20

Weeks went by, and Glenn's legs began to heal slowly. But as they healed, another problem arose. While repairing themselves, the tissues, void of any elasticity, began to tighten and draw up, forcing Glenn's legs to bend back from the knees toward his body, as if being slowly tightened in a great iron vise.

There was no such thing as traction in those days. To keep his legs from drawing back, after the burns had healed, Glenn's mother would massage them for hours. When she was too tired to continue, or had to stop to do other things, Glenn took over, kneading and twisting the muscles and tissues, willing his legs to remain straight.

As weeks stretched into months, the doctor again told Glenn he could sit up, and he stressed that walking would be impossible. But Glenn was determined! Immobile for so long, he found that he was forced to learn to walk all over again. Like a child, he took one halting step after another, using furniture as crutches. Day in and day out, he practiced walking, forcing his legs to move. Eventually he regained full use of his scarred limbs, although it was two long years before he could run even a short way.

But running was something that soon became a natural thrill to Glenn. There was a sense of joy associated with running over the Kansas fields belonging to his father and neighbors. Although the coaches in junior high and high school were quick to notice Glenn's speed and natural athletic skills, Glenn didn't associate running with sports.

Sports was not a subject that arose often in the Cunningham household. Glenn's parents, honest, hardworking people, considered sports a waste of time. There was always too much work to be done around the farm for any youngster to have extra time on his hands.

But Glenn, almost without his knowing it, was drawn to athletics. Five years after the fire, he chanced to walk by the drugstore one day and noticed in the window a display of medals that were to be awarded at the county track meet that weekend. One shiny gold medal particularly caught Glenn's eyes. It was the one that was to be awarded the winner of the mile run.

That weekend, after his parents had gone to town, Glenn mounted a horse and rode to the field where the track meet was being held. Competing were bigger and stronger high-school boys, and had it not been for the several layers of clothes that Glenn was wearing to ward off the late winter cold, he would not have met the seventy-pound-minimum weight requirement.

The little fourth grader gamely lined up with the high-school boys in the race, and four laps around the track later, he crossed the finish line first, winning the first track meet in which he ever participated and laying the foundation for his record-setting mile run that was to come some years later.

The first football game he ever played in was also the first one he had ever seen. Knowing that his parents disliked spoits, the football coach asked Glenn to suit up anyway. Glenn did and eventually played two more games before ever stepping foot on the field for practice.

Upon graduating from high school, Glenn was besieged with scholarship offers. He turned them all down, preferring instead to work his way through the University of Kansas while participating in track. "I felt that if I took a scholarship, I'd owe somebody something after I got out, and I didn't want that," Glenn explained.

Independent as always, Glenn worked his way through college and graduate school as well, while he continued to run in collegiate and AAU track events, setting new records and thrilling crowds wherever he went.

All this from a man who was not supposed to be able to walk again after those terrible burns.

Glenn Cunningham overcame a tremendous obstacle by refusing to give up. When the situation became desperate, Glenn found that when the going gets tough . . . the tough really MUST get going!

"A person must face up to reality honestly as it applies to himself," Glenn explains. "The Lord never made a failure, but often we make failures of ourselves. If we can just pass each test, as it confronts us, we can achieve whatever we set out to achieve."

There is still another side to Glenn Cunningham —a side that is perhaps not as well known as his struggle against tremendous odds to regain the use of his legs, or his fantastic achievement of running the world's fastest mile.

It is a side that shows a compassionate, concerned individual, one who is doing his part to make America a better place in which to live.

Glenn, with his tremendous drive that refused to acknowledge defeat, knows the value of setting goals and reaching them. In addition to the hundreds of honors bestowed upon him for his running ability, he studied and earned a master's degree in education from the University of Iowa. Later he earned his doctorate at New York University. He completed additional courses at Columbia University.

He decided to become a college professor and found a job at his alma mater, the University of Kansas. Then, within a few years, at Cornell College, he was made chairman of his department. During this time, he purchased a small farm of 160 acres. Later he expanded that to 320 acres. He kept adding more and more land to his holdings and through it all his wealth increased.

But Glenn was still an unfulfilled man. To him his success and wealth were but empty victories.

After serving in World War II, Glenn and his wife, Ruth, invited several youngsters who were having problems at home and school to spend a couple of weeks on the ranch with them. He tried in vain to break through the barrier of bitterness and hate that engulfed these selected youngsters like a fog. Then one day he hit upon an idea.

He noticed a boy feeding one of the Arabian horses he raised. The sight of the boy gingerly feeding the animal some grass gave Glenn an idea.

"If you want that horse, he's yours for as long as you stay," Glenn told the astonished youngster. "You're responsible for grooming him. You'll have to feed him and keep him clean, but no one can ride him without your permission. Agreed?"

The amazed boy agreed on the spot, and before long he and Glenn were talking openly about the boy's problems and what he could do to solve them.

This "animal therapy" became a standard method of operation at the Cunningham ranch. As more and more boys and girls of all ages and with all sorts of problems came to the Cunningham ranch, each was given a horse to care for while he or she stayed. Again and again, the animals proved to be the icebreaker needed to open effective communication lines between Glenn and the boys and girls.

Glenn had at last found the fulfillment that had eluded him for so long. The sight of a young boy or girl overcoming bitterness and hard feelings was like a drink of water to a thirsty man. But this natural "high" was not without a price.

The boys and girls stayed at the ranch free of charge. Such an arrangement took a heavy toll on Glenn's finances, and he finally reached a point where his savings were gone and his line of credit was nearly used up. But Glenn never wavered in his belief that God would take care of them. The same brand of "faith" that took him through the potential agony of defeat to the thrill of victory, after the fire, continued to pay off for him. Time and time again, when it looked as though the debt collectors would be knocking on the door any minute, something would happen to remedy the situation.

Thousands of troubled and often unwanted boys and girls have been helped by Glenn Cunningham and his wife, Ruth, and their unselfish devotion to young people. The Glenn Cunningham Christian Youth Ranch has put many boys and girls on the straight and narrow path who might otherwise have ended up in a reform school somewhere.

Glenn Cunningham is truly one of the most dedicated men I have ever known. And his dedication is not for personal gain, but it is an unselfish dedication to help boys and girls who have no place else to turn: youngsters from broken homes, abandoned children, alienated ones. Yes, boys and girls who are desperate.

Through progressive responsibility, work projects, and care for animals, within an atmosphere of Christian love and understanding, Glenn and Ruth Cunningham have been able to help thousands of boys and girls.

Their own investment measured in dollars alone reaches astronomical figures. Their contribution in humanitarian terms is beyond measurement. Your financial help is truly needed if their work is to continue. Contribution checks, large or small, should be made payable to the Glenn Cunningham Christian Youth Ranch, Inc. and should be mailed to the First State Bank, Post Office Box 277, Plain View, Arkansas 72857.

Today, at age 70, Glenn Cunningham is more than an example of determination overcoming adversity. He stands tall as a symbol of courage, honesty, trust in our nation's young people, and trust in Christian principles.

Not too long ago, Joyce and I attended church with Glenn and Ruth and then we had the pleasure of enjoying Sunday dinner with them in their home. It was an exciting day for me to break bread with a man who had been an inspiration to me through the years.

Ask him what his most exciting moment in life has been, and he will answer, as tears come unashamedly to his eyes:"Bringing these kids in and seeing them turn into wonderful, lovable, outgoing people, instead of living in a shell, withered and bittered toward life, is by far the greatest thrill I've ever had."

Today, Glenn Cunningham is busily running the race he has to win. Not for himself, but for boys and girls who have no place else to turn.

3
Turning Scars into Stars

THE NIGHT OF OCTOBER 4, 1969, will linger in Art Linkletter's memory forever.

It is there when he wakes up in the morning, and it is there when he goes to sleep at night. When he stands to speak to almost any of the hundreds of audiences he addresses every year, that date is fresh on his mind.

It's almost as if it were yesterday. And in a way, October 4, 1969, was yesterday for Art Linkletter, so vivid is his recollection of the events that transpired that day.

On October 4, 1969, a twenty-year-old girl, whom many considered to be an up-and-coming young star in Hollywood, jumped to her death from the kitchen window of her sixth-story apartment.

The girl was found to have been under the influence of the drug LSD.

The girl was Diane Linkletter, Art Linkletter's youngest child.

Art was at the United States Air Force Academy in Colorado Springs, Colorado, with his wife, Lois, preparing to speak to the cadets about the evils inherent in an affluent society. Suddenly there was a telephone call. The caller refused to hang up, demanding to talk with Art. He identified himself as Robert Linkletter, Art's son.

Robert had received a telephone call from Diane earlier that evening. She was panicky, screaming something about losing her mind. Robert attempted to calm her, and when she hung up, he ran to his car and raced to her apartment.

He got there too late!

And now he faced the Herculean task of telling his father and mother that their daughter, his sister, was dead.

Art and Lois were stunned and saddened, each experiencing a dozen emotions all at once. His speech was abruptly cancelled as he and Lois hurried back to Los Angeles and to the rest of their family.

At first the full realization of what had happened was too much for Art to bear. How could his daughter have committed suicide? How could she have even used drugs at all? Drugs were used by "bad" kids, or kids who came from broken homes or who were spoiled by uncaring parents. This was not Diane. The Linkletter family—Art, Lois, and their five children— were all close. They did things together, went on vacations together, went to church together. Theirs was a happy, God-fearing home, not at all like the homes of some other Hollywood stars they knew.

Art was devastated. Again and again he wondered how something like this could happen to his family. He had worked so hard all his life to get where he was. From the day, as a baby boy, he was found on the doorstep of a Baptist minister, who adopted him, through his childhood, through his early radio days, and on into the days when programs such as "House Party," "People Are Funny," and "Hollywood Talent Scouts" made Art Linkletter one of the biggest radio and television personalities in the country, he had clung to the belief that right and wrong were two separate, easily identified entities, and using drugs was definitely wrong.

Today, over ten years after that terrible day in 1969, Art can recall that there were signs Diane was engaging in some occasional experiments with drugs, but he had chosen to ignore them.

"I couldn't conceive of it," he told me. "As parents we don't want to believe that it can happen to our kids, and that's often our biggest problem. I figured that with four other kids I knew all about raising children. You develop a pattern of comfortable conformity, and you're not prepared for any difference that might arise."

After the initial numbness wore off, anger set in. Seething anger, coupled with a tremendous sense of loss, had an effect on Art's ability to think and act clearly.

Art was boiling mad, and he stayed that way. He declared an official war on drug users and pushers, especially pushers. These people had killed his daughter by giving her drugs, and he was going to get revenge.

By his own admission Art is not a full-fledged pacifist, but anyone who knows him can readily tell that Art is not someone who enjoys or even entertains thoughts of hurting others. He himself knows that to strike back while in the midst of anger often produces the wrong results.

But now he found himself unable to accept his own advice. The pushers roamed the streets, selling their wares to America's young people, selling drugs to people like Diane, and he was out to put a stop to it. So intense were his hatred and anger and fear that at a closed meeting of the directors of the National Association of Manufacturers, in Boca Raton, Florida, Art threatened to kill another human being.

The object of this hatred was a psychologist and teacher and self-styled guru who preached that LSD was good for people and who built, around the drug, a pseudoreligion that attracted thousands of youthful followers.

At the NAM meeting Art was asked his observations on the drug-abuse problem. Without mincing words, Art launched into an attack on that man, ending his tirade by saying that, "If I ever get my hands on him, so help me God, I'll kill him."

During all this anger, however, Art made one decision that would have a lasting effect on him and his family and would send shock waves through the entertainment colony at Hollywood.

He decided to tell the truth!

Hollywood personalities are taught to always put forth a good face. Life is sweet and happy in tinsel town. Nothing ever goes wrong, or if it does, the public is never to hear about it. That's what press agents are for, to sugarcoat everything and divert inquiries that might lead to unpleasant revelations.

Art decided to forget all that and tell the truth. He told his story to the nation's press, told the country that his daughter had not died from an accident, but had jumped to her death because she was under the influence of drugs.

The reaction was immediate and somewhat frightening.

Rumormongers from "scandal sheet" tabloids immediately pounced on the story and blew it out of proportion. To listen to them, one would think that the whole Linkletter family had been knocked to its knees or that all the children were heavily into drugs. The columnists played on the emotions Art and his family were feeling, writing again and again about their loss. The family's private sorrow suddenly became public.

All that, though, had been anticipated and expected. Art had not been in the entertainment business for forty years without knowing what to expect when something of this nature became public knowledge. But what Art didn't expect was the outpouring of letters from families all across the country who had suffered the same terrible tragedy. Many sympathized and asked him what had gone wrong; where had they failed their children? Others wrote that they knew their kids were involved in drugs and might one day suffer the same fate as Diane. What could they do to prevent it?

But along with these letters came messages from false sympathizers, those who pretended to share Art's grief only to use it as a way hopefully to get Art to endorse their programs which, they felt, would eradicate drug use in no time.

This insult on top of injury only inflamed and confused Art more.

One day a letter arrived that began much like all of the other letters. It, too, expressed sympathy at Diane's death. But this letter went on and asked Art to think through her death and seek from it a purpose, a meaning.

This letter was from Dr. Norman Vincent Peale, and it had a profound effect on Art's life. Dr. Peale urged Art to shape something positive from the ashes of Diane's tragedy. It was a calling card to begin a campaign against drugs, which Art decided to do. To this day, Art believes that God, through Dr. Peale's letter, touched him that day and brought a sense of purpose back into his life.

He had already begun his campaign against drug abuse in this country. But Art's story is far from over.

When he first began speaking on drug abuse, Art's message was that stricter laws for pushers and better educational programs to show students exactly what would happen if they began experimenting with drugs, were necessary.

Police needed to be given full rein, with permission to arrest or club someone on the head if need be.

Art believed that drug abuse was a black and white situation. The kids who used drugs were bad; those who didn't were good. It was the accepted belief at the time, and Art was its foremost proponent.

But as he moved about the country talking to high-school and college students, seeing their reactions, listening to their viewpoints, Art came to the realization that the issue of drug abuse was not black and white, but rather varying shades of gray. There was no quick, easy solution to the problem: no flip phrase that would sum up the answer in five words or less.

It took eight months for Art to overcome his anger and force himself to take a long, objective look at the drug-abuse problem. He found that it isn't always the "bad" kids who are involved with drugs, but normal, everyday-type, intelligent kids who admit to smoking marijuana or experimenting with hard drugs.

Parents are often to blame, either because they fail to discipline or even care about their children, or because they go to the other extreme and are too harsh, too unbending.

But sometimes parents are not to blame. Peer pressure often forces a youngster into drug experimentation. The need to be accepted is strong in young people, and often this acceptance is granted only after drug use becomes involved.

Art was able to channel the energy he had previously devoted to sustaining his anger into learning all he could about drugs and drug users: why they took drugs and where they got them. He visited drug-rehabilitation centers, spent time working as a volunteer on crisis hot lines. He began realizing that his previous "throw-them-into-jail" stance did little to solve drug abuse.

Art has continued his war against drug abuse, but on a much

different level than before. He has served on the President's Advisory Council on Drug Abuse and was president of the National Coordinating Council on Drug Abuse Education and Information. In 1971 he addressed the General Assembly of the United Nations on drug abuse. He wrote a book, "Drugs At My Doorstep," that detailed his experiences and quickly became a best-seller. He continues a hectic schedule yet today, traveling more than a quarter of a million miles each year speaking to various groups, usually about drug abuse.

Wherever he goes, parents ask him for advice in dealing with their children who are often involved with drugs.

Art's answer is simple.

"Attempt to understand the situation as unemotionally as you can. Discuss the situation with your kids," Art advises. "Don't react too strongly. Hear your child out. Don't shut him or her off with an angry display. You'll often find that the problem is a mixture of a lot of things: peer pressure, a desire to be happy all the time. It's a different level of growing up."

Since I have the pleasure of appearing on an average of at least a couple of programs a month with Art, and enjoy an occasional meal with him, I know from personal observations that the tragedy of losing a daughter still weighs heavily on his mind. When discussing it, he becomes quieter, a bit withdrawn perhaps, but never to the point of refusing to discuss it. He decided ten years ago to tell the truth, and though the truth still hurts, it must be told and retold and retold.

A side effect of Art's decision to "go public" with the tragedy and disclose the real truth was the reverberations it sent throughout the Hollywood community. That decision changed the way many Hollywood stars treat the public. Now they are less afraid of telling the truth, less afraid of showing that they are, after all, human and that humans have problems, sometimes serious problems. The recent revelations of Carol Burnett and the battle she underwent to free her daughter from the effect of drugs is but one example.

"My speaking up has given all the rest the strength to speak out," Art told me. "If we take the bows for the good things, we should also show the weaker side of things as well."

The experience of Diane's death has changed Art and his family. For one thing, it has brought an already close family closer. As for Art, he's noticed some changes within himself too.

"I've become more compassionate, understanding, tolerant, religious, and loving. When you see as many people hurting as I have, you have to develop these feelings. Now happiness and satisfaction are the most important things in the world to me."

Art's message to any parent or to anyone who is confronted with the task of picking up the pieces and putting them back together after a devastating tragedy is simple. He tells them, "God has a reason for everything. Sometimes it's hard to find or understand His reason, but we must accept the fact that He always has a reason. We must search for His reason, and then we must set out to TURN OUR SCARS INTO STARS."

Marguerite
Piazza

4
"God, I Dedicate My Entire Day to You"

MARGUERITE PIAZZA moved in a distinctively beautiful way across the stage in Memphis, her strong, clear soprano voice filling the auditorium. My wife and I, along with thousands of other people, sat hypnotized, watching this great performer as she appeared at the Memphis Positive Thinking Rally.

Marguerite Piazza, Metropolitan Opera star, television and nightclub performer who revolutionized supper club entertainment, was to all who watched her meteoric rise to the top of the entertainment ladder during the 1950's, a beautiful, successful woman. But as I listened to her speak that day in Memphis, where I too appeared on the program, I realized that here was a woman who had faced terrible adversity in her life, adversity that nearly killed her. Yet she lived somehow triumphantly through each acid test.

Several months later, my wife and I stood at the front door of Marguerite's elegant mansion in one of the older sections of Memphis. The statuary, the delicate furnishings bespoke a life of quiet dignity and grace. But I was here not to admire her home, but to talk with her and her brilliant husband, Harry Bergtholdt, about her life and her remarkable climb back from the brink of despair.

It all began with a spot on her right cheek. To the layman's eye, it appeared to be nothing more than a blemish, something that is easily hidden with makeup and forgotten. Doctors who would treat her for occasional bouts of laryngitis would tell her the blemish was nothing to worry about, that it would go away eventually.

Too, at the time, Marguerite had worse things to worry about than a blemish. Her second husband, Billy Condon, was in ill health and failing. Already widowed once, with a career that demanded much of her energy and six children who needed attention, the pressures on her were intense. Life held many rude moments for a woman who, to the public at least, seemed to have the world on a string.

Born in New Orleans, Marguerite was raised by her mother and grandmother, her father having been killed in an automobile accident when she was a young child. There was only one rule her mother and grandmother stressed—do whatever you want to do, but do it to perfection.

Even as a young child her performer's blood was flowing. She took dancing, singing, acting, and elocution lessons. At age fifteen she enrolled in Loyola University in New Orleans and within weeks was the top student in the school music department.

Next came New York, which proved to be no tougher than New Orleans to conquer. She literally went from the university stage to stardom, with none of the pavement pounding, door knocking and struggling that most top performers must do before getting a break. She had barely left her teen years when she found herself cast in a leading role with the New York City Opera Company.

The nation's top critics praised her voice and stage presence. And they were often flabbergasted that a woman of such talent could be so beautiful as well. But beautiful and talented she was.

As television started making inroads into people's lives, Marguerite found herself swept up in the commotion. She was signed as a singing star for "Your Show of Shows," which starred Sid Caesar and Imogene Coca and was considered by some as one of the finest shows ever produced for television.

Officials for the Metropolitan Opera Company were quick to notice Marguerite's beauty and talent and soon signed her to a leading lady role with the company, the only star the Met has ever recruited from the ranks of television performers.

Never one to be content with the status quo, Marguerite struck out in a new direction, nightclub singing. But she had more than just singing in mind. Her shows were professionally staged and costumed. Instead of simply going out in front of an audience and singing for an hour, Marguerite incorporated costume changes, choreography routines and dramatic moments into her show. In other words, she created her own "act," something that has now become commonplace among nightclub performers.

There were plenty of down points in her life, however. Her first marriage, which produced two children, ended with the death of her husband. Her marriage to Billy Condon, which produced four children, came to a close when Condon died of heart failure.

But overall her career was still riding high. She had beauty, success, fame and six wonderful children. She also had a spot on her right cheek.

Shortly after Condon's death in 1968, she consulted a doctor about the spot on her face. Tests were taken and the results were frightening. She had melanoma, cancer of the skin. An operation was the only answer.

In an attempt to save her beauty, doctors undermined the skin, removing the cancerous tumor yet leaving the outer layers of skin.

After the operation, Marguerite took her children on a European vacation. Toward the end of their stay, Marguerite noticed a thickening along the scar where surgeons had made the incision. The thickening meant only one thing. The cancer was back.

The vacation was cut short. Marguerite and her children returned to New York. There, doctors confirmed the worse. The first surgery had not removed all the cancer, and this time a radical operation would be necessary. The diagnosis meant her right cheek, the glands in the right portion of her neck, and a large part of her right shoulder muscle would have to be removed. It meant the immediate, violent loss of her beauty.

Overnight she faced the cold, bitter truth that she could be Marguerite Piazza, EX-opera star, EX-television star, EX-nightclub singer. But without the operation she would surely die.

"Your first reaction is that you don't have cancer. Someone else might have it, but you certainly don't," Marguerite said. "It takes awhile for it to settle in, to believe that you truly do have cancer."

But as the truth did take effect, Marguerite found herself agonizing more and more. The mental anguish reached a point where one night she fled from a dinner party given in her honor, racing home to cry hysterically for hours. The thought of ending her life flashed briefly across her mind. But as her children, who came home to find their mother distraught and hysterical, consoled her, Marguerite realized two very important points would prevent her taking that final step. One was the love of her children and the knowledge that they needed her. Second was her inner strength. Her desire to live outweighed any fears of what life would hold after the operation.

The operation was performed and despite assurances by those who saw her, Marguerite knew her beauty was gone. To delay the shock, nurses covered the mirrors in her hospital room. Her Aunt Anne, who was her constant companion, after telling Marguerite how wonderful she looked, completely broke down in the hallway outside her room.

At first, recovery was slow. The operation left her with a slight paralysis which made it impossible for her to pronounce "F" and "S" sounds. But a true performer doesn't let anything keep her from going back to the stage, and four months after undergoing the radical surgery, Marguerite Piazza sang at President Richard Nixon's inauguration.

But that is not the end of the Marguerite Piazza story. There is much, much more.

Marguerite was determined to rebuild her career. But first she underwent nine painful operations by plastic surgeons to remove the scar and repair her face. That done, she faced the next big, frightening step—public performance once again. She finally convinced herself to accept an engagement in Houston, but that night, as she was being introduced, the fears of facing an audience with the knowledge of what had happened welled up inside her. Would they accept her or would they stare at her, trying to see the scar, to discuss later the mutilation that had been necessary?

Somehow she forced herself out onto the stage, where she worked her way mechanically through the first two numbers. But then the applause came, and she realized that the audience was applauding her because of her performance, not because she had lived through a cancer operation.

In 1971 she made good a promise she made when she had her operation. Marguerite devoted the entire year to helping the American Cancer Society raise money for research. She traveled across the country, singing and telling of her experiences. A half-hour film was made of her life, detailing the traumatic effect the sudden knowledge that she had cancer had on her life. The film was introduced by John Wayne, who himself later died from cancer. In all, that year, Marguerite helped raise $70 million for cancer research.

Then in 1974, only six years after her first operation, it was discovered she again had cancer. Fortunately, it was not related to the first cancer. Still, she was forced to undergo seventy-two consecutive hours of radiation therapy in a Memphis hospital, followed one month later by an operation.

And to add even more pressure to an already tension-filled time, came the death of her second eldest son by his own hand.

At first Marguerite was bitter at the news of the second cancer. Over and over she asked, "Why me again?" But Marguerite Piazza is not a person who dwells in a house of despair. She is, to use her own phrase, a "fighter." She is possessed with a tremendous inner strength that refuses to give up, even in the most trying of circumstances.

Marguerite is not one to feel sorry for herself. If a second operation was necessary, so be it. She was determined to live and be a good wife to her husband, Harry, and a good mother to her children.

Ask her how she did it, and Marguerite will answer quickly, "Positive thought, energy, and prayer." She is careful to maintain a proper diet, and with her positive attitude, she truly feels she will never again have a catastrophic illness.

And too, there is her faith in the Lord. She knows that without Him she would never have become an international star. And without Him, she would not be alive today.

"You have to have a desire for life and the will to fight for it," Marguerite says, showing that inner strength that seems to have no end. "You have to have desire to live. Every morning when I wake up I say 'Thank You, God, for getting me through the night. I dedicate my entire day to You. I love my life. I enjoy living, and I thank You for allowing me to live, and I ask You to allow me to live a long time because I want to.' "

John and Greg Rice

5
Two Dimes in a Handful of Nickels

I WAS STANDING in the wing of the stage of the Theatre for the Performing Arts at the Aladdin Hotel in Las Vegas where I was scheduled to speak to a packed house for a Positive Thinking Rally. Also scheduled to speak were Dr. Norman Vincent Peale and others, including two identical twin dwarfs. They were John and Greg Rice, who stood only three feet high. But as I looked down, only John was standing there in the wing with me. My first reaction was . . . run get Greg! He doesn't know it's time to go on.

About that time, Robert Henry, master of ceremonies for the day, said, "Let's give John and Greg Rice a real big Las Vegas welcome." I was too late. Greg simply wasn't to be found, but John went running out from where we were standing to the center of the stage and lo and behold, so did Greg, but from the opposite side, and they both met in the middle of the stage.

What a unique sight! Two identical, twenty-seven-year-old twin dwarfs, three feet high, meeting in the center of the stage, where Robert Henry leaned down to hand them each a microphone.

For thirty minutes they shared with the audience their philosophy of living. Spellbound listeners learned how these two men coped with a life that had to be tough day after day because of the very environment around them —an environment they did not design or build. Normal adults are considerably taller than a mere three feet, and the world is basically designed and built to accommodate the needs of people of normal size. The audience thrilled as they heard how John and Greg Rice relied on positive thinking to see them successfully through each day. Only the day before, at the National Speakers Association Annual Convention in Phoenix, my wife, Joyce, and I had spent the morning with them asking them question after question, compiling their story for this book.

I knew their story was great. I had heard about them before, but I had never dreamed that my respect for them would be so instant. But even more important is the fact that I immediately realized that here was a story that must be shared with the world to give hope and answers to others who would be able to relate to the problems these two men had dealt with since birth.

Needless to say, the thrill of seeing them get a standing ovation caused me to break out with "goosebumps."

The applause started at the rear of the Theatre for the Performing Arts and swept toward us like thunder rolling across the late afternoon sky. Several thousand people were applauding, smiling, and cheering. The noise broke over us like waves pounding the shore. Suddenly hundreds stood, then, just as quickly, hundreds more. Within seconds, all were on their feet applauding.

At that moment John and Greg Rice had to feel ten feet tall. They later told me it was a good experience —truly a warm and wonderful experience, but one that many people thought they'd never know.

Yet here they were, being applauded and cheered by several thousand people in Las Vegas at the Aladdin. People of all sizes, shapes, colors, and dispositions were applauding two identical twins —two identical twin dwarfs only three feet tall.

They told the audience the story of their lives, of a struggle they undertook to overcome preconceived ideas of prejudices, and the effort they put forth to reach a lofty goal they had set for themselves so many years ago. They tell their story not to brag, but rather hopefully to inspire others on to bigger and better things.

Their story began December 3, 1951, in a West Palm Beach, Florida hospital. They told me, "Though each of us weighed about seven pounds at birth, doctors were able to diagnose immediately that we would be dwarfs." The processes that control structural growth and development in the human body just weren't working properly, and therefore they'd never reach even an average height.

They would have the large head and the short barrel chest, common traits in dwarfs. But they would not have a mental handicap; those processes were untouched by whatever affected the growth centers. And although they would always be small, they would have no other physical handicap.

Nonetheless, the news was too much for their parents. One night their father and mother left the hospital and never returned, leaving their two infants to the care and handling of the doctors and nurses.

The hospital of course could not raise them, so they became the problem of state welfare agencies. They were allowed to remain in the hospital while officials searched the entire state of

Florida for foster parents willing to raise not one, but two dwarfs. Officials believed it would be best not to separate them.

Finding a proper home for any foster child is a difficult task at best, but for two dwarfs it is nearly impossible. But one day, after nearly eight months of searching and being turned down, the officials found Frank and Mildred Windsor.

Frank and Mildred lived in West Palm Beach. They were average, blue-collar, middle-class people. They were also deeply religious, especially Mildred, who never missed a special event or service at her church.

Frank and Mildred already had three children, two sons and a daughter, yet something apparently intrigued them about John and Greg. But before they agreed to raise them, they put the matter to a family vote. Did everyone want two dwarfs running about the house? Was everyone prepared for the problems that could result from such a venture?

With much enthusiasm, Greg told me, "To our great fortune the vote was unanimous to take us in, and thus we went to live with Frank and Mildred and their children." He went on to add, "We say 'to our great fortune' because we might have followed a different road entirely had we gone to live with someone else. For with all the love and kindness the Windsors gave us, it should be made clear that they were never allowed to adopt us. Nonetheless, we loved them deeply and consider them our parents. They never forbade us the opportunity to try anything we wanted to try. We might fail, fall flat on our faces, which we did so many times, but we were allowed to succeed or fail on our own. And if we failed, we were allowed to get up and try again.

"Had we been sheltered, pampered, and never allowed to experience failure as well as success, we might never have been able to cope with today's world.

"As it was, we considered ourselves normal kids, no different from other youngsters running around town. Smaller than most maybe, but no different inside.

"Others, however, didn't feel that way. We were to discover, as we grew older, that many people automatically felt we couldn't care for ourselves. The first such problem arose when it came time to start to school.

"Those who controlled the students' destiny in public schools at the time automatically assumed we belonged in a special elementary school designed for unusual children. Special classrooms with specially trained teachers were set aside for children who were blind or deaf or who had had polio or other afflictions. Many of these students were handicapped mentally.

"We didn't have those problems. We were smaller than others our age, sure, but our mental processes were intact. We could talk, see, communicate. Nobody had to carry us around or push us in wheelchairs. We might have to climb up onto a chair while others could sit down on one, but once we got there, we were equal."

John was very emphatic, "We couldn't understand why we were in that special school. We could see and identify the handicap each of the other students had, but we didn't see that we had any. It wasn't as if we were six feet tall one day and only three feet tall the next; we had always been small.

"Fortunately for us, when it came time for us to go to junior high school, there was no place else to go except public school. We looked forward to it excitedly and with a bit of trepidation.

"No one ever told us that dwarfs were supposed to be seen and not heard. So we made sure people always knew we were around. We asserted ourselves, not negatively but positively. We made friends with those who accepted us as people, not as some sort of oddity. When we got to high school, we joined the marching band, both of us playing the cornet. We were very active in extracurricular activities and social events.

"That doesn't mean that life was all smooth sailing. It wasn't. We had many opportunities to become depressed, to retreat into a shell where we could wallow in self-pity and coax others into feeling sorry for us. There have been times when children have yelled on crowded city streets, 'Look at the midgets.' There have been many times when people have made references to midgets they've seen in circus sideshows, 'freak' shows as they are often called."

Greg told me, "We chose not to hear such comments, and certainly not to take them to heart. We didn't feel any different from anyone else, and we saw no reason why we couldn't live like everyone else. As time went on we became more and more determined to live as normal, average, everyday people.

"In fact, we even decided we wanted to go a step better than that.

"West Palm Beach is next door to Palm Beach, the famous retreat of millionaires from every country in the world. When Mom would take us to the beach, we'd often pass these palatial mansions belonging to some jet-setting millionaires. We'd look at the long, winding driveways, the manicured lawns, the yachts docked behind the houses, or perhaps the private plane parked on a private landing strip. Or we'd be sitting along one of the canals that crisscross the countryside in that part of Florida and see a long, sleek limousine pass by, the owner in the rear seat, the car driven by a uniformed chauffeur. We'd look at that and wonder why we couldn't have the same things.

"As much as we loved our parents, they were pure blue-collar people who entertained no thoughts of upward mobility or improved social status. After seeing how life was on the other side of the intercoastal waterway, we decided we wanted some of the better things life has to offer.

"When we were seniors in high school, we attended a lecture by a man named Glenn Turner. Turner headed a very complex operation, and he spoke publicly from time to time, exciting others about making the most out of what they have."

John told me, "We were present at one of his speeches, and we felt as if his words were directed straight to us. We had achieved what we wanted already. But we were like almost everyone else, just average. Now here was a man telling us that if we thought average, we could expect just that—average returns. But if we thought big, we could expect big returns. As he spoke, we thought about the mansions and the yachts and we knew that if we wanted those things, we'd have to start thinking big and working for them.

"We began selling cosmetics door to door during our senior year in high school, and before the year was out, we were doing better than we dreamed possible. It meant long hours and plenty of knocking on doors and pounding the street pavement, but we were starting to see hints of success.

"By the time we graduated from high school, we knew that selling was our ticket to the bigger and better things we dreamed of having. But we had to honor a commitment first.

"One of the saddest moments of our lives was the death of our foster mother when we were in the eighth grade. Three years later our foster father died, as Mother did, of cancer. But before she died, Mom made our brother promise to see that we went to college. Since everyone else in the family labored for someone else, Mom was afraid we'd try to do the same thing, and she knew we'd never last in that world. She hoped that with an education we might be able to survive.

"To honor our mother's last wish, we enrolled at Palm Beach Junior College. Yet the attitude we faced there was the same we had faced countless times before and have faced since. The school guidance counselor told us that even if we got a degree, we couldn't expect to land good jobs. We might not be able to do the work, he said, or company insurance might not cover us.

"We could have gone one of two ways. We could have tucked our tails between our legs and gone away, defeated, or we could show him and others like him that his thinking was all wrong. We chose the latter course of action.

"Ironically, some years later, after we had obtained a reasonable degree of financial success and a modicum of fame, the college invited us back to speak. When we arrived, that same guidance counselor walked up to us, stuck out his hand, and said, 'I always knew you'd make it.'

"With one year of college under our belts, we decided to move on to bigger and better things. We had our future mapped out, and high education wasn't all that necessary. We'd get our degree from the school of hard knocks.

"Our cosmetic sales were going so well that we were offered a job in the home office in Orlando, which we accepted. Once there, we started making public speaking tours, relating our success story to others. We had made it. We had become a success in a big man's world, a world not designed for us.

"In the big man's world, water fountains, light switches, and elevator buttons were all out of reach. Stores rarely had clothes that would fit us. When we bought an automobile at first, we had to buy one with hand controls until we found a man who could modify a regular car to enable us to drive by pressing the accelerator and brake with our foot like everyone else.

"The glamour that comes with constant travel can lose its sheen very fast. We decided to return to West Palm Beach and find a job where we could stay home and sleep in our own beds at night. Plus, we were curious to see if we could make it in another field of endeavor.

"We chose real estate. Some of the veterans in the field

scoffed and told friends we'd never make it, that no one would want to buy a home from a dwarf.

"In our first year in real estate selling, we sold fifty-seven homes, which caused a lot of chins belonging to a lot of veteran real estate salesmen to drop. We did it with determination and positive thinking and by working twelve- and fourteen-hour days. Big thinking requires extra work and effort, but the payoff is big too.

"The news media did several stories on us, some of which went out over the wire services. We have been featured on network television. After a while, as our reputation grew, we started being asked to speak at real estate meetings and conventions. One thing led to another, and before long we again started getting more speaking engagements than we could handle. It was time for a decision: stay in real estate and cut down on public speaking, or go into public speaking full-time.

"We decided to go with public speaking. Once we had been considered below average. Then we made it to average, and now we consider ourselves to be far above average and are thrilled to think that others might benefit from hearing our story.

"Hundreds of people have asked us how we managed to do it. And to all we give the same simple answer. Positive Thinking!

"We never felt sorry for our condition or our lot in life. We didn't use our small size as a crutch to gain sympathy. We didn't use our small size the way many people use their size or color or background as justification for not trying.

"There are no excuses for not doing what you want to do in this world: it is simply a matter of attitude. It's simply a matter of deciding what you want and then setting out to achieve that goal, regardless of what barriers are placed in front of you.

"When people ask us, 'What do you do if you need to use a pay phone?'—we tell them we wait until someone comes along and we ask him to deposit the money and dial the number for us. We're not afraid to ask for help. And if we don't have a dime, we'll ask the guy for change for our quarter too.

"People are a product of their environment. And if they are constantly told that they can't do this or that, then they probably won't.

"We were lucky; our parents never told us that. Yet when we started getting out on our own, others tried to discourage us. They tried to tell us what we could and couldn't do. But fortunately for us, we just never listened. We knew the value of positive thinking!"

That is the story John and Greg Rice tell people wherever they're asked to speak. It was the story they told us in Las Vegas at the Aladdin Hotel, where several thousand people gave them a standing ovation.

> And we know that all things work together for good to
> them that love God, to them who are the called according
> to his purpose.
>
>   Romans 8:28

Both John and Greg told me, "Standing on that stage in Las Vegas, we truly felt the way we always tell people we feel whenever we're asked what it feels like to be little men in a big man's world.

"We always tell them that we feel like two dimes in a handful of nickels. And we do!"

6
From Rule Breaker to Rule Maker

IF I WERE CANDIDLY HONEST, I would admit that the first time I met Dave Yoho he seemed distant, to say the least. The second time I met him, about a year later, he seemed even more standoffish. Now it's hard to become friends with someone with whom you don't feel comfortable. Such was the case with Dave Yoho.

I always work hard, if necessary, at not being guilty of stereotyping a person, and with Dave I felt an immediate problem.

Had it not been for a mutual friend, a fellow member of the National Speakers Association, who straightened out my thinking by telling me about Dave's background, I might have kept my distance and never have gotten to become friends with a man who is not only one of the greatest speakers in America today, but who is also one of the warmest, kindest, most considerate individuals you would hope to meet.

Unless we really know what makes a person "tick," unless we have walked a mile in his moccasins, we have no right to find fault with his or her disposition.

Unless I had known the odor which Dave Yoho had smelled from his jail cell, unless I had known the stench of unwashed men, many sitting in their own filth, mixed with the scent of disinfectant assailing my nostrils and turning my stomach, and the only thing I wanted to do was to run somewhere and breathe clean air—unless I had experienced this, I couldn't possibly have known the deeply planted seeds that had grown to become Dave Yoho's personality.

"The first thing you notice about a jail cell is the smell," Dave confided.

Dave Yoho was in his teens when he first landed in jail. As a tough young kid, he went to New York City searching for trouble. It didn't take him long to find it, and he ended up in jail, standing with perhaps twenty men in the "tank," a large holding cell where arrestees are first held after being taken into custody.

Dave told me, "The others either ignored me or stared at me with silent, brooding eyes, taking stock of the newest addition to their ranks.

"I looked around and noticed that the light bulb in the ceiling had a wire cover over it. Although I had had brushes with the law before, I had never been locked up, and I was curious. So I asked a man sitting on the floor beside me why the wire was over the bulb.

"He was an old man. His clothes were dirty, his beard two days old. He sat staring straight ahead, eyes glazed, evidence of a recent illness still damp down the front of his filthy shirt. A string of obscenities gushed out before he finally answered my question. The wire was there so that I couldn't get to the bulb, break it, and use the glass to cut my wrists.

"I looked around some more and noticed that the toilet was constantly running and the seat was missing. Again a stream of obscenities greeted my question until finally the man answered that the toilet seat was gone so that I couldn't use it as a weapon.

"What class, I thought. I've made the big time now. I've become so bad that I'm not even trusted with a toilet seat.

"But whatever euphoric feeling I might have had at the thought of getting arrested quickly gave way to despair and depression. I soon realized that being in jail was the ultimate shame. It was dehumanizing, and I vowed that when I got out, no one would ever again take away my freedom. Never again would someone tell me when to get up, when to eat, when to go to the 'john,' when to exercise, and when not to exercise. From then on I was going to be a rule maker, not a rule breaker."

That would require a tremendous change on Dave Yoho's part. For most of his life he had been a rule breaker, a street brawler who loved nothing better than a fight with knives, clubs, or bare knuckles.

"I didn't start out a brawler," Dave told me. He went on, "Nor, I'm sure, did my parents intend to raise a kid whose only pleasure in life came from beating others. It just sort of happened that way.

"I was born in Philadelphia in 1928 on the eve of the Depression. My earliest memories are of my father's trying to find work and my mother's serving leftovers until they were all gone. When a family spends every waking moment struggling to live another day, many things get overlooked. Economic pressures have a way of blocking out other problems around you, and so my parents never seemed to notice that their son had a congenital malformation."

The roof of Dave's mouth is not correctly formed, and his

teeth, instead of forming a rounded arch, form a V-shaped one. The right side of his jaw does not lock properly, and one nasal passage is not connected, forcing him, when he speaks, to snort for breath.

The malformation caused a speech impediment similar to that caused by a cleft palate. Added to this was the fact that for the first eleven years of his life, he was grossly overweight. Thus he became the natural butt for the jokes of other kids. After school it became the rage to push his face in the dirt or rip his clothes or mimic him in some way.

Reliving the moment as if it were yesterday, Dave told me, "But if after school hours were bad, the hours in school were worse. Speech therapy was in its infancy when I started school. Every day for several hours, I would join other students with speech problems in a special classroom where we would practice techniques designed to enable us to speak better and be understood more clearly.

"The practice didn't stop when we left the classroom, however. The speech therapist gave my regular teacher instructions to have me speak in front of the class often, and to make sure I used the proper techniques while speaking. For me, it meant speaking with my teeth clenched together.

"Naturally, the other kids in the class didn't know what was going on. All they knew was that here was a kid who spoke with his teeth together, who was hard to understand, and who was sort of fat and funny looking anyway. Their reaction was to laugh, and their laughter hurt deeply.

"The pain might have been soothed if I had received love at home. My mother tried, but with two other kids to worry about and day-to-day living being such a struggle, she just didn't have much time to give. My father shared no love at all with me. There was no communication between us, no touching, no affection. This lack of affirmation, coupled with my other problems, made me feel worthless. I did not feel good inside about myself, about anything. I felt that I wasn't as good as everyone else, and I never would be.

"Although my father showed me no affection whatever, he still strongly influenced my life. When I was ten years old, I saw him take on and beat the neighborhood bully. This memory was to stay with me forever.

"When I was eleven, I started to change physically. The fat gave way to muscle, and I started growing taller. I began to change mentally as well. It was not a conscious decision on my part. Rather, it was something that slowly developed. Then, instead of swallowing insults, I started fighting back when someone tormented me. As with my father, the bullies would find that they had a real fight on their hands when they came after me.

"By fifteen I had developed every aspect of violence known to man. I had found a way to deal with my inner feelings of rejection and nonworth. There was nothing I wouldn't do, no one I wouldn't fight. Before I was old enough for a driver's license I had been stabbed twice in street brawls and had had a tooth chipped by someone wielding a Coca-Cola bottle."

Today, as a result of his face having been punched and broken so many times, many of the bones in Dave's nose and cheeks have been surgically removed.

Dave went on, "Around school I quickly developed a reputation as a guy to avoid. I would fight over the most incidental things. And I fought with a 'no-holds barred' policy. If someone challenged me to meet him after school, my method would be to linger in the hallways for a while, letting the other guy stew a bit. Then I'd saunter out and point out where the battle would take place. But before we ever reached the designated area, I would suddenly turn and punch or kick my opponent. There was nothing I wouldn't do to beat another person, nothing I wouldn't risk to win. My fearlessness came from not caring about myself. My only goal was to smash the other guy into the ground.

"Suddenly I had status. People knew who I was. Those who previously would have taunted me in the hallways or after school would turn and run when they saw me coming. The feeling of someone's jaw against my fist was good, a kick in someone's gut wiped away the bad feelings I carried inside. But only I knew that fighting was but a temporary cure for what bothered me. Later, when I wasn't fighting, the bad feelings would return and be stronger than ever.

"When I say there was nothing I wouldn't do, I mean just that. I quickly developed a reputation of being 'crazy.' On a nickel bet I hung from the railing on the top balcony over the stairwell at school. After going over, I found that I had no way of getting back up. I would probably have fallen to my death had it not been for a girl who told me to swing my legs over to the stairs, where I was finally able to get a hand hold and pull myself up."

On a fifteen-cent bet he inched his way out onto a four-inch-wide ledge over the entrance to a subway and stood looking down at the passersby. Those who noticed him thought he was going to commit suicide.

Yet another time, while standing with a friend, he jumped from an overpass down onto the coal car of a train passing underneath, simply because the other boy dared him to. He did all those things not for kicks, but to be accepted by others. He had been rejected for so long that he wanted only acceptance. And by taking dares, he thought he was finally getting this acceptance. It wasn't until much later that he discovered the truth.

Dave recalled, "I never consciously considered taking my own life. I never thought of falling on a knife or putting a gun to my head and pulling the trigger, but as I look back now, I realize that I was trying to commit suicide every day. I looked for hostility in other people. I went searching for the barroom brawl or fight in a back alley someplace. I vented my hostility, but I didn't really care enough about myself to worry about whether I lived or died.

"There is pain in all growth. Pain is something everyone experiences, and it is something that will never totally disappear. But you can imagine yourself happy or unhappy, and I imagined myself unhappier than most and a person of less worth than others. Call me crazy! So what? When you do, you are only confirming what I already knew. So I hung from balconies and jumped from overpasses simply to act out what was expected of me and hopefully to get from others the acceptance I so desperately needed. That's what put me behind bars in the first place."

Later, Dave entered the maritime service at age fifteen through the use of a falsified birth certificate. But even military discipline couldn't break the mean and careless streak he carried inside. Fights were commonplace, and his shenanigans never ceased.

Dave recalled, "Once we were harbored at the Panama Canal Zone, with orders to remain on ship. It was a hot day and plenty of guys wanted to go for a swim, but orders came down forbidding swimming, citing the area as being unsafe for such things.

"Yet, on a dare, I leaped from the ship's flying bridge into the harbor. The fact that I had only moderate swimming ability didn't even enter my mind. It was a dare and was to be accepted, or at least so I thought. I jumped. But disaster nearly caught up with me. Swift currents whisked me away from the rigging on the side of the ship, and had someone not tossed me a lifeline, I may have been swept away to my death."

It was while Dave Yoho was in the maritime service that he underwent a change that was to have long-term effects on him. And again fighting was involved.

Dave told me, "I was on shore leave in Italy, where we were harbored after being assigned to the Mediterranean. It was a nice, balmy evening, and I decided a glass or two of wine would taste good. One glass led to another, and before long I was pretty drunk, which made me an easy target for a group of local toughs out looking for some fun.

"There were about six or eight guys in the gang. I was walking down a side street on my way back to the ship when they jumped me. It was a short scuffle that ended with them stealing my watch and running away.

"Enraged, I took out after them. Anger propelled me forward, and in a few seconds I clasped my hands around the slowest of the bunch. The rest got away, but I made up for that by beating my poor captive nearly unconscious. I then made a drastic mistake. With the alcohol and anger still controlling my reactions, I took my now bloodied captive to the dockside gates where police were stationed, demanding that he be jailed for stealing my watch.

"I could not speak or understand Italian, and my prisoner launched into a long, impassioned narrative. The more he talked, the more dimly the policemen looked at me. Suddenly one swung a club; then another punched me with his fist, and the next thing I knew I was being pummeled by a dozen or so irate Italians.

"I covered my face and head the best I could, but that still left plenty of areas to hit and kick. Somehow, after it was over and I had been tossed out into the street, I managed to make my way back to ship. The next day I was a mass of bruises from my head down to my groin area. An eye was torn open, my left ear was ripped, my face was swollen, and my gums and teeth were so loose that for two weeks I could consume only liquids.

"I decided then and there that physical violence had to become a thing of the past for me. The injuries were taking too long to heal, and eventually I was not going to walk away from an encounter."

But with that decision that day, a strange metamorphosis occurred, silently, without any sort of conscious feeling on Dave's part.

Though he no longer wanted to engage in physical hostility, the bad feelings he carried inside remained, and he needed to have an outlet for his rage, something that would make him feel good, even if only for a little while.

It wasn't until years later, after he had received a commission in the U.S. Navy, had served with UNRRA, and had built his own sales empire, that he realized what had happened.

"Although I was kicked out of seven different schools for fighting and continued bad conduct before reaching high school," Dave told me, "I was blessed with a quick mind and higher than average intelligence, not to mention a good recall. Twice I was allowed to skip grade levels. After the navy, I entered the selling field, where I used my intelligence and drive to rise quickly to the top. By age twenty-two, I was making twenty-six thousand dollars a year—by current standards equivalent to around eighty-five thousand dollars. By age thirty, I had started my own business, had diversified, and had a net worth of one million dollars. I was married, a father, and lived in a big home with plush furnishings and a swimming pool.

"But to achieve all this, I used something else besides intelligence and drive. I used hostility!

"The physical hostility I had employed during my teen years had unknowingly been transferred to verbal battle. I drove sales teams not only by leadership and motivation, but also by verbal hostility. Many people produced simply because they did not want to fall victim to my wrath.

"I began speaking publicly and conducting seminars. I looked forward not only to the speech but also to the heckler who would occasionally be in the audience. I loved nothing better than verbally to demolish a heckler in front of an audience. In a court of law, I relished being able to do verbal battle with the opposing attorney. When I had 'street' fought, I used to study my opponent for a moment to determine whether he was right- or left-handed, where his strengths were, and where his weakness was. I'd do the same to a lawyer: find the weak point and strike, quick and hard.

"My car became a weapon. Cut me off and I cut you off. Honk your horn at me, and I honked mine back at you. Yell at me, I screamed at you.

"Then one day I came home, and my wife was gone, my children were gone, and the house was completely void of furniture. It was not the first time she had left, but it was the first time she had taken everything with her. Our marriage ended in a bitter divorce.

"About this time I returned to school to study psychology, and as I would read the case histories assigned to us, I began to see that I was reading about myself. This person who was unable to cope with tormentors and turned to physical hostility as a method of handling the situation wasn't some unknown case history; he was me. This guy who flew off the handle at the slightest provocation, who was overbearing, swaggering, and intimidating, wasn't someone in a textbook; he was me.

"Suddenly the knowledge of what I had been and what I had become crashed in on me. I realized that what caused me pain was the very thing people remembered about me. People didn't remember Dave Yoho as a great guy; they remembered him as an abusive person. The hostility that I had made me feel good inside; the crazy things I did thinking others would accept me when in reality they didn't, did not really make me feel good at all. I still had internal feelings of doubt, feelings that I was not a worthwhile person."

Dave started to undergo yet another metamorphosis, but this time the caterpillar turned into something others could like. He stopped measuring himself against everyone else and against the world. He realized that his speech impediment and his intelligence were gifts from God, given to him in His wisdom because of some special plan He had in mind for him.

Dave attributes part of his ability to deal with and accept himself to the Barksdale seminars on self-esteem as conducted by the McGrane Self-Esteem Institute in Cincinnati, Ohio.

Dave told me, "The Barksdale technique enabled me to accept myself and all of my past behavior without guilt, and further established for me a principle of life which was positive in nature and encompassed concepts of family relations, spiritual beliefs, and love of my fellow man."

He believes that discipline was and continues to be an important factor in his life.

Dave went on, "As a youth, I had overcome my speech impediment by discipline, and I decided to discipline myself into being a better person. I accepted myself as a person, but I rejected my behavior. I didn't give up those intangible things that—when whole—make up the body and spirit of Dave Yoho, but I did give up the behavior that caused pain not only for me but for others.

"Today I am happily remarried. I even had an infant son at the age of fifty-one. My wife, Carole, whom I met while still recovering emotionally from my divorce, is one of the most affirming individuals I have ever met in my life. Her actions and behavior have enabled me to accept myself and to radiate a spirit of giving to others that was never possible before.

"My life changed tremendously. Now I devote much of my time telling others who have problems similar to what I had that there is nothing wrong with them as persons. It's their behavior that gets them into trouble. I tell them to do as I did, accept themselves unconditionally. That done, they can then accept others.

"Now, if there is a heckler in the audience, I don't go after him. I know what he's going through, and I can tell him honestly that I know the feeling.

"I have trained over 100,000 salesmen. Many of these have been on long and involved projects, and I have been extremely successful in my role as both a speaker and as a consultant—but unbelievably, once I accepted myself totally and unconditionally, I found that I could release my sensitivities and, in response, the trainees working with me became more productive and more effective in their roles.

"At sales meetings I don't resort to verbal abuse if someone is not doing the job. Now I can honestly tell someone that I love him as a person but that I can't deal with his behavior. On occasion I speak in prisons before groups of tough men who have been through experiences others can't even begin to imagine, and I tell them that God has a plan for them that doesn't include staying behind prison walls all their lives. The trick is finding out exactly what that plan is, be it bricklaying or plumbing.

"I am able to retain my sense of 'physical' being without using physical efforts to either intimidate or coerce others. Exercise, a healthy diet, and a positive and loving attitude are part of my daily practice. Old ways do not die easily and from time to time there is, unfortunately, some slippage.

"I don't have to prove anything to the prisoners. Just because I don't challenge them doesn't mean I would let anyone beat on me or harm me. I tell them that I didn't have to give up any part of me and that they don't have to give up any part of themselves either.

"I now see my early behavior simply as doing the best I could possibly do at my then level of awareness. Yet today, because my awareness has improved and I see things differently, I find no guilt in my earlier actions and no pain from thinking about what might have been. I do not live in the past nor do I concentrate on the pain of my childhood or my unwise behavior."

What Dave did give up was his faulty behavior, and if those with similar backgrounds would release the behavior that got them into trouble in the first place, they would never have to worry about being placed behind bars again.

Today Dave tells them, "Turn from rule breaker to rule maker."

7
"Look at What You Have Left, Not at What You Have Lost"

I HAVE ALWAYS had a soft spot in my heart for children. This soft spot has not been reserved just for my own children and grandchildren, but for all children.

With my father so ill for so many years, I have spent many hours in hospitals. While there, I have invariably seen many sick and injured children; and over the years a special feeling has developed within me for many of these children who never seem to admit defeat, regardless of their problems, but instead struggle to overcome their problems.

I suppose that is why I feel a particular closeness to Carol Schuller, fifteen-year-old daughter of the well-known and respected minister, Dr. Robert Schuller.

Dr. Schuller is the founding pastor of the Garden Grove Community Church and Crystal Cathedral in Garden Grove,

California. His "Hour of Power" television program is viewed each week by millions. It is my good fortune to have the privilege to appear regularly with Dr. Schuller on programs across the country. Backstage, I have felt the warmth that he brings to a room. I have seen audiences "come alive" to his philosophy of "possibility thinking."

Carol is the fourth of five children born to Dr. Schuller and his lovely wife, Arvella. Children whose fathers are ministers often grow up with unique pressures other youngsters simply don't have. Being a "P.K."—preacher's kid—isn't always easy, and in Carol Schuller's case, with her father being so well known and loved all over the world, the pressures could be enormous.

But such is not the case at the Schuller household. The love and respect that engulf all the Schullers overcome any pressure that society might place on any of them.

From an early age, Carol and her brother and her sisters have been taught responsibility and the power of a positive outlook, as well as a love for God. In Carol's case, this training proved invaluable. In fact, it even saved her life.

The evening of July 7, 1978, was a typical summer's night in rural Iowa. The air was warm, the sky was clear, and the evening glistened with the light of a million stars. Carol was visiting her cousins for two weeks while her father and mother were on a trip to the Far East, meeting there with Christian ministers.

Carol and her cousin Mark decided to go for a ride on Mark's motorcycle and enjoy the summer evening. As they drove down the street, Mark driving, Carol seated behind him, a car some distance in front of them stopped and did not pull off the street.

The way was clear, so Mark began to drive around the stopped car. Suddenly, out of nowhere, another car appeared, heading right toward them. It was on them so quickly that

Mark had no time to react. The driver of the second car apparently didn't see them, or else he felt that there was enough room for both cars and the motorcycle. But there was not.

He hit the motorcycle!

The full impact of the moving car hit Carol on her left leg, crushing her against the stopped car and then hurling her like a rag doll off the motorcycle, through the air, and into a ditch eighty-seven feet away. When she landed, the impact snapped the bone in her thigh, forcing the bone through her skin and into the dirt. Blood gushed from the wound and onto the ground. In addition to her badly mangled leg, she was cut and severely bruised over most of her body. Fortunately, she was wearing a safety helmet, which protected her from suffering any brain damage.

Nonetheless, Carol was in serious trouble. As horrified witnesses ran to get assistance, Carol lay in a helpless heap in the ditch, valiantly keeping control of her emotions by repeating again and again the Twenty-third Psalm.

"The Lord is my shepherd; I shall not want."

Eventually an ambulance arrived. But the nearest medical facility with enough staff and equipment for an injury as serious as Carol's was fifty miles away at the Sioux City hospital.

With red lights flashing and siren screaming, the ambulance raced to Sioux City. By the time she arrived, Carol was weak, in deep shock, and very near death. Immediately, doctors started giving her a transfusion. While lying in the ditch and while in surgery, she lost seventeen pints of blood.

Carol was in excruciating pain, but the doctors were unable to give her anything for the pain for fear her already weakened condition would be unable to accept it.

After stabilizing her as best they could, the doctors turned to another problem that required immediate attention. Because her broken thigh bone had ruptured the skin, dirt had been able to get inside the wound. The chance of infection, already extremely high because of the crushed bone, was now inevitable since the wound had gotten so dirty. Doctors washed and cleaned the wound as best they could, and then they made a sobering decision.

The leg would have to be amputated!

Half a world away in Seoul, Korea, Dr. Schuller answered the ringing telephone in his hotel room and received the bad news. Carol was in serious condition; emergency surgery was necessary. Immediately he and Arvella began packing. He would have to cancel his planned appearance at Sunday worship service the next day. A Korean minister, who was on hand as the Schullers hurriedly packed, managed to get them seats on a plane leaving the country that night. He also told Dr. Schuller that the church members would be praying for Carol.

As the Schullers began the long trip east to America, to Iowa, and to their injured daughter, Carol was in surgery. Doctors decided not to amputate the entire left leg but instead amputated that portion below the knee—for now. The rest of the leg was badly damaged in the accident and the damage, coupled with the inevitable infection, didn't rule out the possibility of further amputation later.

As the lonely hours slowly passed, Carol lay in her hospital bed, washed with pain and fear, waiting for her parents to arrive. She recalled what her father used to tell her about how attending church school and reading and studying the Bible were like putting money in the bank—a "spiritual bank." And now, in the early predawn hours of a July day in 1978, Carol Schuller was able to go to her "spiritual bank" and make a withdrawal in faith.

As her father was thinking on the plane, *Play it down and pray it up,* that was exactly what she was doing. She took a second look at what she had left, not at what she had lost. She maintained a positive attitude and spirit. Part of her leg was gone, but she still had her thigh and knee. The pain was tremendous, but she was alive, she told herself. She would make it.

Relatives who were at her bedside in the hours before the Schullers could arrive marveled at Carol's spirit. Instead of a down-and-out, defeated feeling, Carol remained positive in her outlook.

Such an outlook was not easy to maintain as the hours stretched into days and the days into weeks. As expected, her leg became badly infected. Doctors were unable to close the wounds. They had to let them remain open so that the infection could drain out. The regular changing of bandages was an extremely painful experience, and Carol could not keep from crying out.

She was forced to remain in traction at all times. The metal traction devices painfully cut into what was left of her leg; her back became sore from constantly having to lie flat.

With the infection came a fever, and at times, when thinking of her softball team or of water skiing or of riding her horse, Carol would for a moment or two lose her brave vigor and her positive attitude. Her faith would desert her just for an instant, and she would cry out in pain and fear and self-doubt. Then, in a matter of seconds, she would recover her poise and faith. "Things might be bad now, but they could be worse," she'd say.

Carol was helped to a great extent by her father and mother, who alternated keeping a bedside vigil the entire time she was in the hospital. The rest of the family, her brother and her three sisters, immediately ceased whatever they were doing when they heard of Carol's accident and made their way to Sioux City. The love that had bound the family together for so many years now became even stronger, thus enabling Carol to maintain a positive outlook and a strong faith in God.

Too, she began getting telegrams. President Jimmy Carter sent one, as did Senator Edward Kennedy, whose son Teddy had had to have a leg amputated because of bone cancer. John Wayne, Billy Graham, and Steve Garvey of the Los Angeles Dodgers, all sent telegrams expressing their sorrow and concern and urging her to recover quickly. She received telegrams and letters from all over the country.

Immediately, Carol began setting new goals for herself. One of her first goals was to raise herself up from the bed by grabbing hold of the bar hanging above her. Another goal was to see how long she could go without requesting pain killers.

She constantly needed intravenous medication, and nurses often had trouble finding a vein in which to place the IV needle. Again and again nurses had to excuse themselves from the room after having jabbed Carol's arm time after time, attempting to find a vein for the needle. So Carol made it her goal not to cry out when the nurses started sticking her arm in search of a vein.

Carol had no appetite, and by not eating, she quickly started losing weight and strength. So it became her goal to eat four bites of everything she was served each meal. And as the days went by, more bites were added to that goal.

Still, the biggest fear hanging over Carol was the possibility of another operation to amputate the remainder of her leg. Carol quickly adopted the positive attitude that doctors would not amputate her leg so long as she felt, and God agreed, that it would not be done.

Carol was soon transferred from the Sioux City hospital to an advanced medical center in Orange County, California, near the Schullers' home. There, doctors performed some exploratory surgery on Carol's damaged leg and concluded that, while the healing would be painful in the interim, further amputation would not be necessary.

Carol was elated and immediately began thinking of a prosthesis and what she would be able to do. Eight weeks after the accident, doctors were finally able to remove the sutures that had closed the end of her amputated leg. Nine weeks after the accident, Carol was taken out of traction. The shock of being able to see fully, for the first time, her partially amputated leg sent Carol into a deep depression. Yet with her religious upbringing, she soon regained a positive outlook about her tragic experience and about her life in general. Soon she had a new motto: "I can't wait until tomorrow."

She began planning for physical therapy, learning to walk with the use of crutches and eventually with a prosthesis. Fortunately, her spirit became more positive than ever, and later she was to need every bit of the strength that her positive attitude provided. When she left the hospital, more than two months after the accident, Carol's homecoming was tempered by the doctors' demand that further surgery, the fifth time since the accident, would be required.

Carol was determined that this would be her final surgery and that the doctors would decide once and for all not to amputate the rest of her leg. With this positive spirit of mind, Carol went back into the hospital and later, after the surgery, came back out the same person she was when she went in. Doctors had indeed decided that everything was satisfactory and no further amputation would be required. And, as Carol had already decided, that was the last time she underwent an operation on her leg.

One of the goals Carol set herself was to be able to walk down the aisle at her sister Sheila's wedding. It was a goal she kept.

She had to use crutches, but she proudly made her way down the aisle on the day of her sister's wedding, bringing tears to the eyes of all who were there.

After she was out of the hospital for good, Carol began physical therapy to rebuild her strength and to learn how to use the prosthesis device she now wears. Before the accident, Carol was an active teenager who was constantly on the go. She played on a girl's softball team, she loved to water ski and snow ski, and she loved to ride her horse. While she was unable at first to return to school and had to have a tutor come to her home, Carol was determined to be once again the active person she had been before the accident.

This she has accomplished. As hard as it might be to imagine, once again she enjoys feeling the cold winter breezes on her face as she races down the side of a mountain on skis. That's right. Carol snow skis, prosthesis and all.

She attended a special ski school located in Winter Park, Colorado, which teaches physically handicapped youngsters how to ski. I have been there myself and have marveled at the amazing work done at this school. Handicapped youngsters, some with prosthesis devices, some without, ski like professionals down the side of the mountain. Many are on just one ski, but they enjoy those moments on the mountains more than anything. And there among them, from time to time, is Carol Schuller, thrilling once again to the excitement of snow skiing.

All of this has not been easy. Carol has had her moments of depression, moments when everything seemed bleak.

But Carol is made of stern stuff, and her low moments have never lasted long. She springs back more determined than ever to get on with living a normal, happy life.

She is once again active in the church, belonging to the youth groups and singing in the choir, making further deposits in her "spiritual bank" for withdrawal at a later date.

On occasion she writes to other youngsters, some older than she, some younger, who have suffered serious injuries that will leave them changed for life. She relates her experiences and how she managed to overcome one of the biggest obstacles that anyone can face. Helping others is not necessarily a ministry for Carol, but rather it is something that she does out of a love for other human beings. She doesn't deliberately set herself up as a model for others to emulate; she is much too humble for that. But anyone who has met and talked with her, as I have, knows that Carol Schuller is a real inspiration to other teenagers. Maybe God did plan a special ministry for her after all.

Carol simply tells others, "Look at what you have left, not at what you have lost."

8
From a Great American Family

IN THREE SECONDS Ben B. Franklin went from climbing mountain peaks to struggling over bedpans.

In less time than it takes to read this paragraph, Ben's life did a triple somersault that forced him to completely readjust his physical and mental capabilities. It was an unasked for change, and the change wrung many painful, agonizing moments out of him, but in the end it may very well have been necessary.

It was April 14, 1963. Ben was mountain climbing with two friends who were fellow classmates at the University of Colorado. The three had spent the afternoon practice climbing on the walls of the Amphitheatre, a small rock formation near Boulder.

Ben's companions were on a ledge above him, and Ben was climbing the last few feet to join them. It was to be their last climb of the day. Instead, it became the last mountain climb Ben was ever to make.

Suddenly, without any prior warning, the rope Ben was holding broke, sending him plunging 150 feet to the base of the cliff. Upon impact his back broke in four places, his pelvis in two. Somehow, miraculously, he didn't die.

His companions climbed down as fast as they could to help him. But even so, it seemed an eternity until the ambulance finally arrived. Ben, nearly drowning in a swirling whirlpool of pain, could say or do nothing as the ambulance attendants carefully loaded him onto a stretcher and placed him in the ambulance for the thirty-mile trip to St. Joseph's Hospital in Denver.

At the hospital, doctors immediately started operating on Ben's back, carefully repairing the vertebrae that had been broken and dislodged. After four hours on the operating table, Ben was sent to recovery. Now only time would answer the one question everyone had but dared not ask.

Would he ever walk again?

Temporary paralysis is not uncommon in the sort of injuries Ben sustained. But after four days had passed and Ben still could not move his legs, feet, or toes, doctors knew the worst had occured. Ben was paralyzed from the waist down. He was eighteen years old.

It seemed so unfair, so wrong, that somehow he, who more than anything loved the mountains and who trembled with excitement on every summit he reached, was now unable to move. Initially, Ben refused to believe that the accident had truly occurred. It was as if he were in a dream, that the broken rope, the fall, the cold night breeze being pierced by the screaming sirens of the ambulance, had not really happened.

The first time Ben saw the Rocky Mountains he was nine years old, and he had never seen a more majestic sight. As the summer slowly passed and the other boys at the camp were busy learning archery and riflery, Ben spent every spare moment walking through the mountain forests, enjoying the peace and solitude they offered. Ben found that he was fascinated by the beauty of the trees and the animals, that he felt cleansed breathing the sweet air after a summer shower. Sleep was never so restful as in the quiet mountain forest, lying on a bed of pine needles, the moon and stars for a blanket.

Ben went back to the camp the following summer and for every summer the next seven years. He began learning the art of mountain climbing, and he discovered that scaling the rugged mountain sides, jumping from rock to rock, thrilled him as nothing before had done. The lessons were not without pain, not without the occasional bumps and bruises, but Ben found that the exhilaration of standing on a mountain top, looking almost as if from heaven on the countryside below, was worth every hardship it took to get there.

And now, all that was behind him, forever gone. Before him lay a life spent in a wheelchair. He would never walk again.

And yet, the first time I met Ben he stood up and shook my hand. When the doctors predicted that he would never be able to move without benefit of a wheelchair, they didn't know the real Ben Franklin. The real Ben Franklin's vocabulary does not include words such as "never" and "impossible."

When I first met him, I was immediately impressed by the courage and determination that lay behind his pleasant demeanor. I was further impressed when later I learned that Ben had not only conquered the wheelchair, but he has become a world traveler, visiting places few others have dared go. At the same time, he manages The Associated Clubs, a successful speakers' bureau.

He has traveled up the Amazon River in a dugout canoe, crossed the desert on the back of a camel, and made his way through the Indian jungle riding an elephant. While others who shared a fate similar to Ben's would be feeling sorry for themselves, Ben was watching the secret ceremony of a king being cremated on the island of Bali.

The inevitable question Ben is always asked is whether he is related to the Ben Franklin so proudly recalled in American history books. The answer is yes. Ben B. Franklin is a descendant of the patriot Ben Franklin. Just as "old Ben" was courageous and determined, so too is Ben B.

But it was not always that way. For weeks after the accident, Ben refused to believe he would no longer move his legs as he once had. He spent countless hours playing and replaying the accident in his mind. Why was he there in the hospital? He asked himself again and again. Why did the rope break?

Eventually he turned his anger to God, blaming Him for allowing the accident to happen.

Two separate feelings overwhelmed Ben the first few weeks after the accident: depression and frustration. The depression was accompanied by a sense of futility and despair, the frustration with anger.

"The grimmest day I ever spent was the day I discovered, while eating a meal off a tray in the hospital, that I could move my fingers and thumbs at will with no effort at all but couldn't move my legs," Ben told me. "I wanted to move my legs so badly but I was powerless to do anything."

Three weeks after the accident, doctors transferred Ben to the Craig Rehabilitation Hospital in Lakewood, a suburb of Denver. Here doctors taught him how to roll over and how to drive a car with hand controls.

But they could do nothing about his mental attitude, which was now working against him. For the first six weeks of his hospitalization, Ben remained in a prone position. He loathed the thought of any sort of rehabilitation and yet as he lay in bed, his legs were rapidly degenerating. In extreme cases such as

Ben's, the patient sometimes experiences what is called spontaneous regeneration. In other words, the affected limb somehow heals itself, forcing strength and power back through the muscles, making the limb useful again.

But for Ben, unless he was able to summon some sort of movement quickly, his legs would eventually reach the point of being totally useless.

Ben eventually turned to God, realizing that God was his only chance of obtaining any degree of recovery. Yet he found that he was unable to keep anger out of his prayers. It would spill out in bitter words and warm tears. But in retrospect, Ben believes God expected the anger because it was an honest feeling.

"I think getting angry at God is completely natural, and I think God would be disappointed in you if you didn't get angry," Ben explained to me. "It's a completely honest feeling, and the secret to effective prayer is complete and total honesty. If God bores you, tell Him so. He wants all of you, not just the pleasant parts."

Honesty is just one part of the healing process, Ben believes.

"The other part of the recovery process is total acceptance of God's will. It's not your will but His will that counts. Once you realize that, the recovery process is complete.

"I remember that one day I prayed 'not my will, but Thine be done,' and I really meant it. The next day I moved a toe. It was six weeks after the accident, and people at the hospital told me they had never had anyone go beyond four weeks without movement and still experience some spontaneous regeneration. But I went 50 percent longer than anyone else and still had some regeneration.

"I got more joy out of moving that toe than reaching the highest summit in the world."

Lest anyone think such acceptance of the Lord's way is easy, let Ben assure you it is not.

"For me the physical recovery began about six months after the accident, but the emotional recovery took much longer. Emotionally, I started recovering in late summer when I faced reality. All other avenues had been closed, so I tried the avenue of acceptance, to make the best of the situation. But this process of acceptance is a painfully long one, and even though you accept reality fairly quickly, it takes a long time, about two years, to get your subconscious to really mean it and be thankful for it.

"It's easy to mouth the words," he told me, "but it's really meaning it that revolutionizes the whole thing."

Yes, when we begin to accept the Lord's will and when we can believe that His will is best for us, then our fears and frustrations begin to vanish.

> . . . Be not afraid, only believe.
>
>   Mark 5.36

In retrospect, Ben believes the turning point of his whole life was his decision to stop trying to control his own destiny and let God impose His will.

"That moment of total acceptance, when I was completely willing to accept His will even if it meant remaining in a wheelchair the rest of my life, turned out to be the key to the whole victory," Ben said. "It's the only way you can survive. You might not be religious going in, but you will be coming out."

This victory was not without a price, however. A steep price. For Ben found he was forced to rethink and restructure his entire life. He admits to being a bit cocky and bigheaded before the accident. A particular phrase he used whenever he passed a test or accomplished a goal was "this is a day for dancing."

Following the accident, that phrase became especially bitter for him because now he couldn't dance.

With mountain climbing and other physical diversions suddenly cut off, Ben turned his attention and energy to other activities such as school work and debating and public speaking. He found this forced reorientation of his life excruciating. Changing one's ideas and thought processes after eighteen years is not easy. He wanted to be independent, but he found he had to learn to accept other people's sympathy without becoming angry, because they meant well.

It was a battle, but Ben managed to win.

When Ben was a boy, his father, perhaps unknowingly, planted a seed in the back of Ben's mind. Slowly over the years the seed germinated and grew and in 1964 finally came to fruition. Ben decided he was going to do something he had wanted to do for a long time —travel about Europe.

Ben had been released from the hospital in time to resume his studies at the University of Colorado. During long hours spent reading textbooks, Ben would occasionally dream about traveling through Europe and even seeing the Matterhorn, which he had once hoped to climb. But sitting at a desk in the dormitory thinking about something and actually doing it are two different things. And as the end of the school year approached, Ben became more hesitant about going.

Doctors at the rehabilitation hospital, while not wanting to deny Ben every possible hope, were not convinced Ben would be able to move about on crutches for extended periods of time. The most he had been able to stand with crutches had been two hours.

The day Ben was to leave for Europe found him sitting in his wheelchair at the base of the ramp leading up into the airplane. But with a final jolt of determination, Ben grabbed his crutches and made his way up the ramp and into the airplane to his seat. It was June 1964, fourteen months after the accident, and when his plane left the runway, Ben said goodbye to his wheelchair forever. To this day he has never again sat in a wheelchair. He moves about with the use of crutches, leg braces, and a back brace.

At first, Ben wondered if he had made the correct decision. The first two weeks in Europe were almost more than he could take. Europe, with its castles and cathedrals and towers, all of which have hundreds of steps, is not enticing to a person on crutches. But despite the pain, Ben managed. The more places he went, and the more he did, the more his confidence developed.

Since those first halting, fearful steps, Ben has become one of the most widely traveled people in America.

He has not shied away from hardships. In fact, he has welcomed them. Even though he will never regain full use of his legs, and must always use crutches, Ben still is able to do about 80 percent of the activities a totally healthy person can do.

Thus he has felt the warm breeze of the Amazon jungle on his face while traveling in South America. He has braved the hot, choking desert, clinging to the back of a camel, and ridden a horse through the Colorado high country. He has been around the world six times and has visited 112 foreign countries and nearly every exotic locale known to man.

His travels started as a hobby. But as he continued to visit various countries, he discovered that traveling was both a recreation and a means of bringing his life into sharper focus, with the help of the Lord.

Too, he finds that each day is a new adventure, every hour a new discovery.

"I find that the longer I live, my talents seem to exfoliate," he told me. "They open like a flower. I've found I have a talent for writing, public speaking, and lecturing. I think it's made me a more embraceable person."

In 1966 Ben visited the Mayo Clinic. He underwent exhaustive tests, and the findings were that he has more mobility and development than a person as extensively injured as he was has a right to expect.

Much of it has to do with attitude, with a positive mental approach, Ben believes.

"I visited a ward in the hospital once where quadraplegics and paraplegics stay and they absolutely amazed me," he said. "I'm talking about the ones who have been paralyzed for years. There was no bitterness. Their attitude was tremendous. I found that 80 percent of the people do overcome traumatic accidents, while the other 20 percent seem to wallow in self-pity."

Ben knows how low a person can feel whose life has been drastically and tragically altered. The lowest moment in his life came not immediately after the accident, but twenty-one months later in January, 1965.

He had just returned from another trip to Europe and was having some disagreements with his girlfriend, disagreements that eventually led them to go their separate ways. Ben immediately blamed the trouble on his accident, feeling that if he were not paralyzed, things would have been different.

Even today, sixteen years after the accident, Ben has periodic bouts with depression. And as anyone who has suffered with emotional distress can tell you, conquering emotional problems is harder than overcoming physical handicaps.

But Ben has never allowed himself to fall into the trap of self-pity. When depression strikes, he takes strength from the knowledge that God will make sure it passes.

Many have undoubtedly suffered problems similar to those Ben experienced. Perhaps problems that are even worse in comparison. I asked Ben how a person keeps from giving up totally, from allowing self-pity to overcome and eventually end his life.

Ben points to two key elements:

"First, you have to accept the fact that what's happened has happened. You are where you are. You can't deny reality. You have to start there and not where you want to be.

"Second, remember Christ's words that a person must lose his life to find it. You have to be drawn together from the outside. You must give in order to receive. You must give your life to Someone who is much bigger than life itself."

Earl
Nightingale

9
"Stay with It"

MILLIONS OF PEOPLE have heard Earl Nightingale and have been helped by the uplifting messages aired on his daily radio program, "Our Changing World."

More than one thousand radio stations in North America and abroad carry Earl's program as a part of their daily broadcast schedule. An estimated thirty million people tune in each day to hear what Earl has to say. But how many people have actually been helped? How many have been pulled from the brink of despair by the infectious answers this profound, gentle man puts into his daily messages? It is impossible to say, A hundred? A million? Three million? No one keeps statistics like that.

But imagine, if you will, the rut in which some of these people might still find themselves if Earl had listened and believed what others were telling him when he first conceived the idea for his own radio program.

Earl's story is a bit different from the others in this book. Some of the chapters deal with people who have overcome a tremendous physical or mental handicap and gone on to achieve greatness in their chosen endeavor. Some had known the sweet taste of success before fate suddenly took it away. Yet they persevered, got tough, kept going, and climbed back to the top of the mountain, arriving better persons than ever before.

Earl, though, has a slightly different story, but one that carries a vital message nonetheless. His is a story of overcoming apathy, disinterest, and misconceptions on the part of others, and of believing in himself and a dream, and working to achieve that dream.

The year was 1950, and the place was Chicago. Young Earl Nightingale had achieved his goal: he was working as an announcer for a major radio network, CBS. But as with so many dreams we often have, reality never quite equals our imagination.

And so it was with Earl. He had worked long and hard to reach the plateau on which he found himself. But now that he was there, the plateau wasn't all that great.

At CBS he was announcing the news, interviewing celebrities, hosting musical programs, in short, doing everything but what he wanted to do, namely to write and deliver his own show. Seeing the situation as hopeless at CBS-Chicago, Earl followed the only option open to him. He quit.

He decided instead to form his own company and write his own radio broadcast. He needed just one thing—sponsors. And he would have to find them himself.

But sponsors were nowhere to be found.

As luck would have it, when Earl started looking for sponsors to pay for his radio program, television was just beginning to capture the American public's fancy. Advertising executives and other "insiders" immediately started predicting the end of radio. Why should anyone want to listen to radio, when he could both see and hear on TV?

Sponsors left radio for television like rats deserting a sinking ship. Radio stations were almost to the point of begging for sponsors. In the midst of all of this, Earl would rise early on the cold, gray Chicago mornings, and set out down the street, stopping at every business and advertising agency that might possibly agree to sponsor his program.

The days were long, the turndowns many. For the first few months, the first year in fact, the going was extremely rough. Had it not been for the "Sky King" radio show, in which he portrayed Sky King, Earl would have been hard pressed to keep body and soul together. As it was, life was pretty shaky.

But it was during those bleak and dreary times that Earl developed a philosophy that has seen him through many rough and depressing moments.

When I was visiting with him in his home in Florida, I asked him if there was anything he did when he got depressed and the world seemed to be against him instead of on his side. His answer was a simple three-word phrase.

"Stay with it!"

"Stay with it," he said. "That's what I tell myself when it seems the world is falling in on me. Things will work out.

"I'm a writer, and I get in a depressed mood now and then. I think that, from time to time, all creative people do. But three or four days later, I find myself feeling great and happy again. The problems vanish. They have a way of taking care of themselves.

Earl is the first to admit that this philosophy does not fit every situation. There are times when a reassessment of one's position and goals is necessary, but if the goals are right, and if one believes in them, then he should stay with it.

Staying with it is what got Earl through those first threadbare
months when everyone was interested in advertising on TV
and no one was interested in sponsoring a radio program.

Earl did stay with it, and he found enough sponsors to pay for
a fifteen-minute radio program on Chicago's WGN. As more
and more people started listening, the program time was expanded and then expanded again and again until soon it was
one of the top radio shows in Chicago.

Earl is a man of seemingly limitless energy. Just as his radio
program started going strong, he added a daily telvision program to his busy schedule. Then he founded his own insurance
agency. Within two years the agency rose from last to sixth
place in sales among the several hundred agencies in the
company.

In 1956 Earl made headlines in newspapers everywhere by
announcing his "retirement" at age 35. He didn't retire in the
commonly accepted sense. Instead, he devoted his time to
research and study to find out what motivated people. And it
was at this time he wrote and recorded "The Strangest Secret."
This masterpiece was a thirty-minute narration in which Earl
outlined his proved plan for success.

"The Strangest Secret" became the most popular "talk" record of all time, winning the gold record award for sales in
excess of one million copies. Even today Earl gets letters
thanking him for the powerful, life-changing message the re-
cording contains.

Earl joined forces with his good friend Lloyd Conant and
formed the Nightingale-Conant Corporation, of which Earl is
chairman of the board. The company is one of the largest and
most successful producers of audio and video cassettes and
films for training and self-development.

In 1959 Earl began a new syndicated five-minute daily radio
program, "Our Changing World." This program has since

touched countless lives and has steadily grown throughout the free world.

So far it sounds as if Earl has had a pretty easy time of it. A few rough spots here and there maybe, but overall pretty easy.

Well, that's not quite so. When Earl was ten years old, his father left him, his mother, and two brothers to fend for themselves in Los Angeles. It was 1931, and the Depression was at its deepest. Before long the Nightingale family found themselves living in a tent city in Long Beach, California, trying to stay alive while living under a piece of canvas stretched across a wooden floor.

It was a hand-to-mouth existence, and Earl sold newspapers and did any odd job he could find to bring in some money.

During all of this, he became a very curious youngster. He wondered why it was that so many were in such bad financial shape. Since most of his neighbors were adults, and since adults supposedly knew everything, he asked them.

No one knew. No one could tell him why the world had suddenly plunged to such a low ebb.

"I thought adults were supposed to have the answers to the problems," Earl recalled. "Yet the ones I talked to had very few answers, if any. So I decided I would find them on my own, and I started reading as my search began. The answers just had to be in a book someplace."

So it was that Earl introduced himself to a public library and to reading. It was a momentous introduction, for Earl has never stopped reading. His thirst for knowledge was unquenchable, and it still is for that matter. By his own admission, he overcompensated for his desire to gain knowledge. He read constantly. And books are still his best friends.

Yet, as a young boy, his best "friends" could not help him find enough money to buy an ice cream cone for his favorite girl friend, nor could his newly found "friends" help him buy some

new clothes so that he could look nice at high school graduation, an event he decided to forego.

After high school, Earl joined the Marine Corps, and after
service overseas in World War II he was sent to Camp LeJeune
in North Carolina to serve as a training instructor. After military service, Earl attended the University of Oklahoma, where
he studied creative writing under Professor W.S. Campbell, at
the time, the nation's top creative writing instructor.

While he was stationed at Camp LeJeune, in the Marine
Corps, Earl found a part-time job with a local radio station. This
training served him well and later enabled him to get a radio
job in Phoenix, Arizona. He diligently worked to improve his
broadcast delivery, earning the teasing nickname "network"
from his fellow employees because of his insistence on sounding like the top network announcers.

But his drive for perfection paid off. When he decided to
make the move to Chicago and to big-time radio, he was ready.
He auditioned for NBC and CBS. Both offered him jobs. He
choose CBS. Some might call Earl lucky, but getting a network
job and later establishing his own successful program fits in
with Earl's definition of luck.

"Luck is what happens when preparedness meets opportunity," he said.

"We determine our own circumstances," he adds. "If you
find that the circumstances are not going to lead you where you
want to go, then change the circumstances."

For some, who hear his voice only on the radio, Earl might
seem like a man who has gotten rich by telling other people
what they can do to make their lives better. But anyone who
has met Earl and known him over the years, as I have from
appearing on programs with him, can tell you he doesn't say all
those things because they sound nice. He says them because he
knows, from personal experience, that they work. His life
copies his words.

Four years ago Earl developed arthritis in his hips. The left hip became so painful that the bone was surgically removed and replaced with one made from titanium. But unless he told you about it you'd never know. Earl never complains or seeks pity because of his problem.

"People need to remember that everyone faces problems," Earl said. "Problems are pretty much the same for both successful and unsuccessful people. It's just that successful people learn that problems can be solved.

"And to solve a problem, a person needs to remember just one thing: Stay with it."

Mary
Crowley

10
"Trust in the Lord"

PRETTY SOON, after you keep on hearing so many nice things about someone, from so many people, your curiosity starts to get the best of you.

Through the years, I have repeatedly heard so many heartwarming stories about a wonderful Christian lady by the name of Mary Crowley, founder and president of Home Interiors and Gifts, Inc., that I decided that I had to meet her for myself.

Most of those telling me about her were women who were attending my memory seminars around the country. They were happily engaged in bettering their place in life, for themselves and for their families, by working with this Dallas based firm. Many of these women had moved from low self-esteem and a gross lack of self-confidence to the realization that where there's a will, there really is a way.

109

As these women learned of my personal interest in helping others find themselves through self-understanding, they were quick to step forward after the seminars and tell me about this marvelous woman.

There are many rags-to-riches stories, and certainly Mary Crowley's is one. But her life, and the tragedies and triumphs it has had so far, goes far beyond a simple success story. So much has happened to her during her lifetime, so many potentially traumatizing moments, that hers is a truly remarkable story.

Earl Nightingale once remarked that all people face problems. It is just that some find ways of overcoming their problems while others are paralyzed into bitter self-pity.

Mary Crowley is one who solves her problems. She is a spirited, brave, and loving woman whose secret of succeeding and overcoming even the most devastating problem stems from one unshakeable belief:

Trust in the Lord.

This simple statement is also one of the most difficult directives to understand, believe, and follow. But as Mary explained to me, trusting in God means total trust, even when the situation appears hopeless or confused. Mary's advice is not to waste time trying to figure out God. Just trust in Him. The key is trusting in God to care for you even when His way seems confusing.

Mary's advice stems from personal experience. Many times in her life she has had to trust in the Lord even though she didn't understand what He was doing.

A happy, enjoyable childhood is something all children should have and most parents hope and pray their children will enjoy. But the cold, plain fact is that not all children are blessed with a loving, happy childhood. Mary Crowley was one such child.

When Mary was eighteen months old, her mother died of pneumonia, and Mary was sent to live with her mother's parents on their farm near Kansas City, Missouri. Her father set out for parts unknown. Mary's sister and brother were sent to live with other relatives.

Life with her grandparents, whom she soon started calling Mama and Papa, was rich and full. They were loving, hardworking people who taught Mary the importance of work and trusting in God. They also instilled in her a sense of self-confidence, something she was soon to need desperately.

Her father, a school teacher, later remarried and settled in the state of Washington. He sent for his children. Mary had come to deeply love and admire her grandparents and the home they made for her, and she was frightened and confused about moving so far away to live with a father, a brother, and a sister she barely knew, and a woman she did not know at all.

Children sometimes have the ability to sense an uncomfortable situation before it happens. Mary came to her new home with a sense of foreboding that quickly proved to be warranted.

Mary's stepmother cared little for her or the rest of the family. She never cleaned the house or cooked. When it was discovered that Mary's grandmother had taught her to cook, she was placed in charge of the kitchen. Mary soon began to resent her father, who seemed oblivious to the cruel way his wife treated the children.

One year Mary worked hard picking fruit and vegetables in order to earn enough money to buy a beautiful red coat she had seen in a catalog. Finally, after weeks of work, Mary had saved up enough money. She gave the money to her stepmother and showed her the coat she wanted her to buy that afternoon in town. When her parents came back from shopping, her stepmother carried into the house a brown coat with worn sleeves and tassels hanging down the back. It was obviously used. In fact, it had come from a rummage sale. Instead of buying the red coat with the white fur collar Mary had so desperately wanted, her stepmother had purchased a cheap, used one, saying she would keep the rest of the money for Mary's school expenses.

So cruel was Mary's stepmother to her and her brother and sister that the three children sometimes prayed she would die.

Finally, when Mary was thirteen years old, concerned neighbors reported her stepmother to the authorities. Later, she was declared an unfit mother, and the children were taken from her.

Mary and her sister went to live with their grandparents. But Mary's grandparents had moved from their Missouri farm to Arkansas, and while they were as kind and loving as ever, Mary was restless. She wanted a home that was really hers.

Her desire for a home of her own was so strong it blotted out practical considerations. While in high school, she met and fell in love with a fellow student. They were married immediately after graduation and soon were the parents of two children, Don and Ruth. Unfortunately, Mary's husband was incapable of accepting the responsibility of a wife and family, especially since the Depression was upon them and day-to-day living was a struggle.

By the time Don and Ruth were ages three and one years old, the family had moved to Sherman, Texas. The family was so desperately in need of money, Mary decided that the only recourse was for her to go to work. She left the children with a neighbor, put on the best dress and hat she owned, and set out looking for a job. She walked into the fanciest department store in town, walked straight to the owner's office, and announced that she was ready to begin working.

The owner smiled sadly and gently informed her the Depression was on and he could barely pay the employees he had. No job openings existed. But Mary, naive about the working world and filled with the self-confidence given her by her grandparents, refused to take no for an answer. Instead, she got him to agree to let her work one Saturday, and if she didn't sell enough to pay her salary, he need not offer her a job. The owner accepted, sure that Mary would be in for a rude awakening.

Saturday came, and by the time the last customer had left the store, Mary had sold more than any other saleswoman, including those who had been at the store many years. The owner was impressed and offered her a job.

Even with all her hard work, Mary's wages weren't enough to support two growing children. She needed a better job making more money, and the only place such an opportunity existed was in Dallas, one hundred miles away. Mary had always dreamed of being an accountant, but that required education beyond high school. While Dallas was home for several fine universities where she could take accounting courses, where would she get the money to pay the tuition?

One day Mary learned that a local Rotary Club gave an annual $100 scholarship to a needy student for further education. Although she was older than most applicants, Mary decided to apply for the scholarship anyway. To her delight, she was chosen recipient. The money meant that she could enroll in a business college in Dallas, but it also meant that she would have to spend most of her time away from her children. It was a hard decision to make, but one that Mary felt was necessary.

So for a year Mary spent weekdays in Dallas going to school and weekends in Sherman, working at a local department store and seeing her children, who were staying with friends.

After finishing business school, Mary found a job with an insurance company. She was able to bring her children to Dallas and hire a maid to care for them during the day while she worked. Her young husband had meanwhile joined the Army and was going his own way, and a divorce seemed inevitable. Money was still a scarce commodity. But in spite of the fact that

Mary barely made enough to cover the month's bills, she decided to tithe. Since moving to Dallas, Mary had joined the First Baptist Church. She wanted to tithe desperately, but the economics of the situation seemed to deem otherwise. However, after much praying and reflection, Mary decided to tithe anyway. She decided to trust in the Lord because somehow He'd make sure everything was all right.

And God did watch out for her. During the month when more money was especially needed, God somehow found a way that Mary could work overtime, thus earning extra money. With the money supply tight, both Don and Ruth were forced to begin working at an early age. Her neighbors gossiped about and condemned her, but in subsequent years, Mary realized that the early introduction to work made her children good, hard-working, dependable employees.

In 1948, Mary met and married David M. Crowley, Jr. Their marriage was a happy union of two loving souls, but it soon created conflict within the family. Mary's son, Don, not used to another "man" around the house, felt threatened by Dave's presence. Tempers often flared, but Mary's cool, calm, responsible, yet sensitive, handling of the situation soon enabled Dave and Don to become friends.

In 1949, a momentous incident in Mary Crowley's life took place. She was introduced to the world of direct sales. She attended a house party at which different waxes and cleansers were shown and demonstrated. By this time Mary had become an accountant for a Dallas furniture store, and when the woman demonstrating the products suggested that Mary consider becoming a direct saleswoman, Mary simply waved her hand. After all, she had a steady, secure, relatively well-paying job. But she was astounded to learn that the direct saleswoman earned more and was doing a job she obviously enjoyed.

Mary decided to try the direct selling on a part-time basis.

Before long, she was making more money selling cleansers and waxes than as an accountant. She quit her accounting job and began selling full time. Soon she was making more money than ever before, but the best part was that she was truly enjoying every minute of it. What Mary didn't know was that while she was enjoying her work, she was also laying the foundation for skills that would serve her well in the future.

One day, after Mary had established herself in the direct selling field, she received a telephone call from a local importer of gifts and decorative items. The importer could get the merchandise into the country, but he knew nothing of establishing a direct selling business. Would Mary come to work for him?

It was a startling call, but after much consideration, Mary realized that she must accept the challenging offer.

One of Mary's most solid beliefs is that a good home goes far in keeping a marriage strong. And a good home begins by looking good. If she could help other women make their homes look good with decorative items, then she would be doing a great service.

Mary spent three years organizing and building the company. By 1957, the company was financially sound and enjoying continued growth. About that time, however, the owner decided to cut back on the bonuses paid to sales managers who had worked hard to build a territory. Too, at one special vacation trip, the owner planned a cocktail party.

Being a strong Christian, Mary disdains the use of alcoholic beverages. She also believes that money earned is best spent helping others and should not be hoarded. She wrote a memo outlining her beliefs to her employer, hoping to avoid further conflicts. His reaction was negative, so Mary offered to resign.

At 7 o'clock the following Monday morning, the doorbell at Mary's home rang. Outside stood a man with Mary's desk, chair, and filing cabinet, which she had purchased herself. No thank you's, no personal explanations, no nothing. Just her desk, chair, and filing cabinet.

Mary was reduced to tears. One day she was vice-president of a growing company; the next she was unemployed. Suddenly it seemed that she had nowhere to go, no place to turn. Her husband, Dave, soothed her as best he could, but Mary's hurt was very deep and bitterly painful.

At this, the lowest ebb in Mary's already hurt-filled life, God helped her and showed her the way again. Something inside Mary told her to dry her tears and set out on her own. Recognizing God's signs, she did just that. She dressed in her finest clothes and set out to see the suppliers who dealt with her former employer. All were delighted to learn that Mary was considering forming her own company.

Next she talked with a lawyer friend, who explained the regulations connected with forming one's own business. In just one day, Mary went from being unemployed to seeing the nucleus of building her own company, which she called Home Interiors and Gifts, Inc. Her family—husband, Dave, son, Don, and daughter, Ruth—encouraged and helped in the business. Son Don is now a motivating factor in the company's success.

Establishing a company and making it successful are two separate things, however. Mary worked many long, hard hours, giving demonstrations and decorating shows, and recruiting "displayers," people who would sell her accessories on the hostess plan. She faced discrimination—after all she was a woman, and banks were reluctant to give loans to women in business, especially one which had housewives as associates. But Mary persisted and eventually found a bank that would lend her the money she needed.

Throughout, Mary operated from a set of firm principles. She wanted associates who were physically attractive, emotionally stable, financially intelligent, intellectually awake, and spiritually dynamic.

At many of her home hostess parties, Mary noticed that the women often seemed to lack self-confidence. If any of these women decided to work for her, Mary was determined to instill self-confidence in them, along with the knowledge that God comes first in everyone's life and career second. She did not, and still does not, urge women to give up their families for a career. Quite the opposite. She believes that a good family life is important, but it shouldn't prevent a woman from having her own career if she chooses.

After two years of hard work, Home Interiors was well established and operating smoothly, which is more than Mary could say for herself. Always overflowing with energy, Mary found herself becoming more and more fatigued. Eventually, she decided to consult a doctor. His diagnosis was heartstopping.

Cancer!

The test for any true Christian is adversity. When times get rough and the future seems to hold nothing but uncertainty, faith is put to the ultimate test. And so it was with Mary. But she had been a believing Christian much too long to forsake God now. If she had cancer, there must be a reason. Or if not, then she could be cured. Mary underwent painful radium implants and cobalt treatment, and the cancer was eventually brought under control.

Meanwhile, Home Interiors was going very well. In 1962, the Home Interiors sales team realized one million dollars in sales, only five years after the company had been formed.

Then trouble began. On November 22, 1963, President John F. Kennedy was assassinated in Dallas. Sadness and anger swept the country. Somehow, in seeking an excuse, something or someone to blame, the country seemed to settle on Dallas, where the tragedy occurred. Suddenly Home Interiors rallies in some states were cancelled. Sales people quit, all because the company was headquartered in Dallas.

On the heels of this problem, Mary's daughter, Ruth, who had married and moved to New Jersey, gave birth to a baby boy. Mary flew there to be with her daughter and grandchild and to attend a Home Interiors rally. The baby was only a day old when it contracted a staph infection. The next day, the child died.

Through the years, problems continued to confront Mary.

In 1977, while flying his personal plane back from a ski vacation in Montana, Mary's son, Don, crashed on landing at a Dallas airport. His wife and three children were only slightly injured. Don, however, suffered severe injuries to his head, face, and foot. Immediate surgery was necessary. The risk of infection was high, and no antibiotics had been developed that could counteract that particular type of infection.

Through all her past turmoils, Mary had never forgotten God. Once again she prayed to God to protect Don in his hour of need. And again, God answered her prayer. Don survived the surgery and today is completely healed.

There have been many bright sides to Mary's life too. In 1974 she became the first woman to serve on the board of directors of the Billy Graham Evangelistic Association. Soon the Dallas Chamber of Commerce and the Direct Sales Association also asked her to serve on their boards. There too, she was the first woman ever asked to those positions.

Through the years Mary's faith in God and her perseverance have paid off.

Home Interiors began to show a profit. Today it is a multimillion-dollar company and sells millions of dollars worth of merchandise each year and numbers associates of over 30,000 people, mostly housewives. Many of her saleswomen came to her afraid and unsure of themselves. Today they have confidence and trust in God, thanks to Mary's teaching.

In 1977, Mary was invited to the White House, along with twenty-four other national business leaders, for a conference with President Carter and his Chiefs of Staff. In 1978, Mary received the Horatio Alger Award, which is presented to those who have faith in the American free-enterprise system and who have shared their fortune in such a way as to present jobs, health, and a high standard of living to others. Mary has done this and more, for in addition to the thousands of housewives she has helped get started in business, Mary and Don established Handi-Hands, a company operated completely by handicapped people. She also helped former Olympic gold-medal winner Paul Anderson establish a home for boys in trouble with the law in Dallas.

Her exciting books, *You Can Too* and *Women Who Win,* published by the Fleming H. Revell Company, have helped thousands of women throughout America deal with their identity crisis by enabling them to discover that they can find fulfillment with a challenging career and, at the same time, by living according to Christian principles, become better homemakers, wives, and mothers.

To name all of Mary's projects and involvements would take far too much space. Suffice to say that she is living a full and meaningful life, despite the many pitfalls that were waiting to trap her in a morass of self-pity.

As I sat across from Mary Crowley in her Dallas office, I asked her what her advice would be to those who find themselves in a situation where it looks as if the entire world is against them.

Her answer was simple and to the point:

"Trust in the Lord!"

*Charlie
Plumb*

11
Six years a POW

I LOOK FORWARD every year to attending the National Speakers Association Annual Convention.

Besides inspiring and instructive seminars, I enjoy meeting old friends I never see any other time.

During the convention in 1977, I was, as usual, looking to find some old friends to sit with during one of the more exciting seminars.

The master of ceremonies for the hour asked everyone to find a seat so that the program could begin on time. Unable to locate any old cronies, I quickly grabbed a place on the front row and sat down between two strangers.

Beside me sat a man I immediately sensed was somehow different from anyone I had ever met before. I found my attention drawn to him, as if some big, unseen magnet were pulling at me. I judged him to be in his thirties. He was slight of build, not particularly tall, with a receding hairline. But most of all, I was conscious of a tremendous strength emanating from this quiet, rather harmless-looking human being.

Perhaps it was his eyes and the way he seemed to look through you, searching out every deep secret you hoped to keep hidden your entire life. Maybe it was the tightness around the mouth. Whatever it was, this man radiated a quiet assuredness that comes only after experiencing something few others have, like a long, grueling test which only a handful of people pass and many fail.

The man, I learned later, was Charlie Plumb. And he had, as I suspected, endured an ordeal many have undergone but few have lived to tell about. For six years Lt. Comdr. Joseph Charles Plumb, Jr., U.S. Navy, was a prisoner of war in a North Vietnamese prison camp.

His is a story of years spent in a man-made hell on earth. It is a story of beatings, physical and mental torture, humiliation, and deprivation. It is a story of tremendous risks, risks that endangered his life and the lives of many fellow POWs.

Above all, though, it is the story of one man's tremendous faith in God, a faith that withstood the barbs of mockery and accusations by captor and fellow captive alike—a faith that refused to crumble even while suffering the lowliest existence a man could have.

From the day Charlie was born, God played a large role in his everyday living. Every Sunday would find the Plumb family in church, studying Scripture, singing hymns, and listening to the sermon. At the age of thirteen, Charlie attended a church camp. After the service, the minister asked if there was anyone who wanted to receive Christ into his life. If so, he should come up to the altar.

Without so much as a second thought, Charlie went forward and received Christ. At that moment he made a commitment to God, and since he was strong-willed even as a youngster, it was a commitment he never forgot.

One might think that Charlie, having suffered as he did, would be a melancholy sort of person, laconic, perhaps even sarcastic. In fact, he's not. When I was able to talk with him privately after the seminar, I found him to be bright, friendly, and humorous.

"Humor helped me a lot in Vietnam," he told me. "I think that even in adversity, people should try to find something to laugh at. It just seems to make things easier."

The sun was turning the morning sky brilliant hues of violet and blue when Charlie took off from the aircraft carrier *USS Kitty Hawk* the morning of May 19, 1967. In the back seat of the F4B Phantom's cockpit sat Charlie's radar intercept officer, Gary Anderson.

Charlie had been on Vietnam duty a year. But in just five days he would be leaving the *Kitty Hawk* for a refresher course and a trip back home to his wife and loved ones.

The mission that day was to bomb an area south of Hanoi in North Vietnam. As the squadron approached the target, adrenalin started flowing through everyone's veins. The North Vietnamese had sophisticated antiaircraft missiles, and one mistake could be fatal.

Five thousand feet below, the Vietnam jungle was a green blur as Charlie piloted his jet toward the target area. Suddenly there was a thump and a jar in the rear section of the plane. The instrument panel was instantly awash with red blinking lights. The plane rolled upside down and started diving toward the ground. Flames shot from the tail, turning the plane into one huge, flaming bomb.

Cold sweat broke out on Charlie's forehead as he tried to right the aircraft. The plane would not respond. The controls were jammed.

Wildly the plane sped toward the ground. Ejection was impossible because the plane was inverted and the force of the ejection would hurtle both men into the rice paddies below. For one horror-filled second, it seemed as if the two men's lives would end in a massive blast of fire and smoke.

In desperation Charlie put all his weight on the rudders, which, miraculously, still worked. Slowly the plane righted itself, and Charlie and Gary were able to eject.

On the way down, hanging beneath his parachute, Charlie ripped apart a special book he carried which contained the names of the pilots in his squadron. He also took time to say a quick prayer, thanking God for sparing his life and asking Him for strength to endure whatever waited below.

When he landed, angry peasants quickly surrounded him, stripped him naked, and herded him off to the nearest North Vietnamese army officer. The officer loaded Charlie, who had been permitted to put his shorts back on, into the back of a jeep. Blindfolded, Charlie lay in a bruised and battered heap as the jeep bounced along the road toward Hanoi and the "Hanoi Hilton," as the pilots had dubbed the POW camp.

At the camp Charlie was taken to a small room and made to sit in a wooden chair. It didn't take a genius to figure out what was going to happen next. Charlie mentally prepared himself as best he could.

A North Vietnamese army officer entered, followed by two guards. Quickly he began asking Charlie for military and political information. Charlie refused to cooperate. The officer threatened torture. Still Charlie refused to answer questions, knowing his answers would be used for propaganda purposes. The officer left, and two more North Vietnamese entered.

Manacles were put around Charlie's ankles. His arms were forced behind his back and manacles placed on his wrists. The manacles, adjustable so as to conform to different size wrists, were tightened severely, so severely that circulation was cut off and Charlie's hands turned greyish-blue and numb.

A rope was wrapped around Charlie's elbows and drawn tight, stretching the shoulder muscles and straining his sternum. He was knocked to the ground, trussed with wire, and forced into painfully awkward positions, his head touching his ankles, his wrists high up on his back. The guards kicked and pummeled him with their fists again and again.

Eventually, the torture stopped and Charlie was again asked questions. Exhausted, beaten, nearly unconscious, he avoided further torture by giving false answers to the questions asked. Finally the officer and guards left, but the torture had really only just begun.

After a sleepless night, Charlie was shoved into a dark, eight-foot-by-eight-foot cell. It was here he would spend the next several weeks. Later he shared a cell with another POW, and still later he was one of fifty-seven men in one cell. But at first he was kept in solitary confinement.

"Time passes slowly," Charlie told me, "when you are alone in a dark, tiny cell with no window or light. Before long your mind starts wandering: panic sets in as you fearfully start thinking about what might happen to you next.

"So often we hear comments about how 'time flies.' But if you have ever sat and stared at a clock for a full sixty seconds, you realize just how long a minute really is."

Charlie knows. Frightened and alone in that small, dark, humid cell, he became painfully aware of just how long minutes can be and how slowly it takes those minutes to stretch into hours and hours into days.

Stories of POWs going "stir crazy" are not uncommon. Being

deprived of contact with other human beings, being forced to remain silent, and being unable to tell whether it is day or night quickly affects a person's mind. Hallucinations often occur. Charlie was aware of this possibility, and he worked to avoid succumbing to the pressures being purposely applied by his captors.

"I concentrated on remembering every church service I ever attended," Charlie told me. "Then I went through all the hymns I had ever heard sung and all the sermons I had heard preached."

It quickly became apparent to Charlie that if he was to survive the ordeal he was now in, he would have to have a reason for living, something that would continue to spark a desire to remain alive. That reason was provided by the Lord.

Like a beacon on a foggy night, or food and a warm bed to a lost and wayward traveler, the Lord gave Charlie something to cling to during those terrible dark hours. He was the unseen but ever-present force that accompanied Charlie everywhere and gave him strength to face another day. Like a stranded mountain climber, clinging to a lifeline, Charlie clung to this world on the strength of his religious faith.

About two weeks after his capture, Charlie was sitting in his cell when he heard what at first he thought was a cricket. But as the sound continued, he realized it was a scratching noise coming from inside his cell. Closer investigation revealed that the source of the noise was a wire poking through a small opening in the wall of his cell.

Charlie pulled on the wire, and the person on the other end pulled back. Charlie pulled again; the other person pulled back, this time taking the wire away.

In a few minutes the wire returned with a minute piece of paper attached. Listed on the paper was the alphabet in rows and columns with the instructions to "memorize code, destroy note."

Charlie followed the instructions and soon was communicating with the unseen person at the other end of the wire, a person he eventually learned was Lt. Comdr. Bob Shumaker, who had been a POW for two and a half years before Charlie arrived.

Slowly, letter by letter, word by word, the two men communicated. With the benefit of his experience, Shumaker told Charlie what he needed to survive in a POW camp. It was an admonition Charlie still carries with him today. Simply, Shumaker told Charlie he needed faith in God, commitment to life and country, and pride. Man is built in the image of God and God didn't design man to fail. There was, Shumaker said, no alternative. It was either follow these three points or be buried on Communist soil.

Like John on the prison Isle of Patmos, there are times in life, if we are to sustain life, that we must be able to call on a power far greater than any power on this earth.

> ". . . behold, I have set before thee an open door, and no
> man can shut it. . . ."
>
> Revelation 3:8

Another thing Shumaker told Charlie was that church service would be held on Sunday. Charlie's heart leaped for joy at the idea of an organized service. But when Sunday came, nothing special happened. The guards went about their business as usual; the POWs remained in their cells. About noon Charlie heard five forced coughs, what Shumaker said would be the sign that service had begun. Suddenly Charlie realized what Shumaker meant. The North Vietnamese did not believe in God, and any worship would have to be done privately in the individual cells. This weekly church service, private as it was, made survival possible.

After several weeks of solitary confinement, Charlie was moved to another section of the "Hanoi Hilton" where he was jammed in with other POWs in small cells.

It was an improvement over what he had before, or at least as much an improvement as a POW camp could offer. But something more was needed, he realized.

At the Naval Academy, Charlie had belonged to a Christian organization known as the Officers Christian Union, a group whose main pupose was to train men to serve as chaplains aboard ship. It was an entirely volunteer organization, but Charlie enjoyed belonging.

So Charlie soon found himself serving as chaplain to fifty-four POWs. Actually there were fifty-seven POWs in the cell area, but three claimed to be atheists and wanted no part of the service. Instead, they acted as lookouts, sounding a warning when guards approached.

"After 1970 our treatment improved," Charlie recalled. "We asked for a Bible, but we were refused. So we went on a hunger strike until they gave us one.

"Finally the Vietnamese gave us an old tattered copy of the Bible they let us keep for two days. Where they got it I don't know, but the effect the Bible had on the men was amazing. Many just wanted to touch it, and the first ones in line were the ones who said they were atheists."

Charlie told me, "I doubt if the three men were true disbelievers. By the end of our captivity they were attending services regularly. In fact, I know they are regular churchgoers today. I feel they were believers all the time, but they were just afraid to step forward and admit it."

Having the strong faith and commitment to the Lord which

Charlie had didn't make day-to-day living in the prison camp any easier. It just made it possible.

The POWs were subject to continued interrogation and beatings. For the first three years of his captivity, Charlie remembers, the Vietnamese dreamed up reasons to "purge" the ranks of the POWs. A communications network was established among the POWs in different cell blocks. This network was vital to the POWs well-being, and Charlie was instrumental in establishing secret codes. But detection by the North Vietnamese brought instant, painful reprisal.

One day Charlie was caught looking through a vent attempting to make contact with another prisoner. Such action was strictly forbidden under camp "regulations," and his being caught warranted the "fanbelt" treatment, as the POWs nicknamed it.

Charlie was taken into an empty room, stripped naked, and forced into a spread-eagle position on the floor. Guards stood on his hands and legs while other guards beat him with eight-foot-long rubber whips cut from old tires. Twice he was subjected to such torture. The scars remain today.

It is easy for a person to say he has a deep and strong faith in the Lord. But it's another thing to have it tested daily for six years, as Charlie did.

> But he knoweth the way that I take: when he hath tried me. . . .
>
> Job 23:10

Even though his love for the Lord was strong and constant, Charlie was still subjected to the humiliation, the fear, the loneliness, and the frustrations of being a prisoner of war in a far-away country. The Vietnamese were always thinking of new ways to further add to the POWs' heartaches. They delighted in showing the POWs pictures of Americans demonstrating against the war by burning their draft cards or vandalizing government buildings.

Even when the Vietnamese started allowing limited mail privileges, the news from home was not always good. Charlie was one of those who was allowed to write a short, sterile letter to his wife every month or so. He was allowed mail in return, but only after it had been closely read and at times censored.

But one day a letter arrived that compounded Charlie's misery. His wife could no longer cope with the separation and the constant fear of what was happening to him and the agony of wondering if they would ever again be together. One day, the pressure became too much, and she wrote Charlie that she was filing for divorce.

Even at his lowest, most difficult moments, Charlie never abandoned his faith in God. It would have been easy, as others did, to question the Lord and His ways, even to forsake Him. But Charlie never did.

The Lord knew of Charlie's deep, abiding faith and one day gave him a sign to bolster his spirits. It was after Charlie had been beaten yet another time in what prisoners called the Green Knobby Room, a room specially designed to muffle the screams of tortured POWs. It was here, while lying on the floor in sheer burning agony, Charlie looked up to see a Christ-like shadow on the wall. It was a sign that the Lord had not forgotten him.

In fact, Charlie even considers his confinement to have been spiritually beneficial. He was forced into a period of deep personal reflection. It was a time of introspection, of deciding exactly what was and was not important in his life. Separated from material wealth, Charlie still had something to cling to: his faith in an unchanging God.

In 1972 American and North Vietnamese leaders signed the famous Paris Peace Treaty. America's involvement in an unpopular war half a world away drew to an end. The POWs were coming home.

After being away from home a total of seven years, Charlie found he had to make a tremendous readjustment. He found he had to reacquaint himself with plain day-to-day living. But the memories of his confinement would not fade away.

He decided to put what he had learned as a POW to use in helping others. He became a public speaker and has appeared at seminars, conventions, and meetings, and before boards of directors of large corporations, sharing what he learned during his dreadful confinement. Charlie has authored three books and currently guest lectures several times each week. For more information you may write him at P.O. Box 223, Kansas City, Missouri 64141.

Since first meeting Charlie, I have appeared on stage with him. I have heard him tell the audience the importance of faith in God. I am proud to call him a friend.

Everywhere he goes Charlie is asked if he has words of wisdom for people who find themselves in desperate situations, for people sitting in their personal, small, dark cells. His answer is always the same. Harkening back to the long years he spent as a POW, Charlie tells people the things they need to overcome any hardship: "Everyone needs faith; a commitment to personal ideals, society, and country; personal pride; self-discipline and humor."

W. H. "Bill"
Burden

12
When the Great
Scorer Comes

IT WAS SATURDAY, March 31, 1979. Joyce and I had spoken that morning at the Vita Craft convention in Kansas City.

As we always do, at least once each day, we went to a pay phone and called to see how Dad was doing. When we called the day before, he wasn't doing very well. This had been one of his longest stays in the hospital.

The minute I heard Mother's voice, I knew something was seriously wrong. She said, "Dad's slipped into a coma."

Crying, she went on to say, "Please come as soon as you can. I'm not sure you can make it in time now."

Even before I hung up the phone, I was praying. Mother had been through so much, and I didn't want her there alone if Dad passed away.

Those at the convention were saving a place at the table for us for the noon meal. We rushed in and excused ourselves, then hurried to our motel room, threw things into our suitcase, and headed for the Kansas City airport.

Luckily, the next flight for Tulsa left shortly, and we were on it. We taxied out to the end of the runway on board Braniff's flight 237 and were ready to speed down the runway for takeoff.

But suddenly the stewardess's voice came over the public address system, "Ladies and gentlemen, the pilot has just informed me that we are going to have to taxi back to the gate. There is a malfunction in the hydraulic system. We hope the delay won't be too long."

But the delay was long. In fact, the stewardess finally came back on the public address system with yet another disheartening announcement.

"Ladies and gentlemen, rather than wait any longer for repairs, we are being transferred to another plane. Please make sure you have all of your 'carry-on' items. Your luggage will be transferred. We are sorry for the added delay."

This couldn't be happening, I thought. Not now; of all times, not now.

But it was happening. Joyce and I desperately needed to get to Tulsa, and it seemed that everything was working against us.

We finally got off the ground over an hour late. The whole time I could hear Mother's words—"Please hurry."

When we got to Tulsa, we still had to rent a car and drive the ninety miles to Sedan, Kansas. The minute we got on the ground in Tulsa, I rushed to a pay phone to call Mother again at the hospital. She seemed relieved that we were only a little over an hour away. She asked us to drive carefully because she knew we'd be driving faster than we should.

My main concern was still to be with Mother so that she wouldn't be alone. Somehow, this concern was uppermost in my mind.

The trip up Highway 75 to Bartlesville seemed to take

forever, and then the road from Bartlesville on to Sedan seemed to have no end. When we got to Sedan, we rushed straight to the hospital and to Dad's room.

The Sedan City Hospital was almost home to Dad. He had spent so much time there.

He looked as weak, as pale, as fragile, and as bad as he had ever looked to me. Mother and the nurses told Joyce and me to do what they had been doing. Talk to him. Shake him. Do anything that might bring him out of the coma. His eyelashes were actually becoming matted from his eyes being closed so long.

Between Joyce and me, we did everything. I think one of us was shaking him or talking to him constantly. We finally persuaded Mother to go home and get some rest.

There was an extra bed in Dad's room, and about 1 A.M. Sunday morning I talked Joyce into lying down to get a little sleep. I finally sat down in a chair at the foot of Dad's bed. But most of the time I was either rubbing his forehead, shaking him, or talking to him—anything and everything, trying to bring him out of the coma. But all to no avail.

About 3 A.M., mentally worn out, I sat back down in the chair at the foot of Dad's bed. And then it hit me. I couldn't bring Dad out of that coma, but I knew Someone who could.

God could!

Calmly, I said, "Okay, Lord, we've tried to wake him. We've failed! Now, in the name of Jesus, I pray that You will open his eyes."

I had never in my life had the proverbial "bolt of lightning" come down out of the sky and strike me. But I was a believer. Otherwise, I suppose I would never have known that it was time to ask God to open Dad's eyes.

I'm forty-eight years of age, and for the first time in my life a bolt of lightning DID come down from a mighty God above and strike me.

Within ten seconds by the stopwatch, after I had said that prayer, Dad opened his eyes. I must confess that my first reaction was disbelief. He kept them open about five seconds, and then he closed them.

But he did open them—or did he?

My second reaction was, *You're seeing things.* So I got up out of the chair and stood over him. Then, to me, an absolute miracle happened. Again, Dad opened his eyes for about five to ten seconds. Then he closed them and kept them closed for the next thirty hours.

Now I have good eyesight, and I can see. Although I was tired, I knew that I wasn't "cracking up." Then it really hit me.

Friend, God just sent down that "bolt of lightning" to prove to you once and for all that He does hear and answer prayers.

I knew right there and then that Dad would make it. And still today I can see and feel the miracle as it happened that night.

Little did I know that less than fifteen hours later they would have to rush in the "crash" unit, as they called it, give Dad a shot to keep his heart beating, place a mask over his face that forced him to breathe and do all kinds of things when it looked as if he were gone.

That was around six o'clock Sunday evening. Around eleven o'clock that same evening he stopped breathing again. This time Mother started sobbing hysterically, "He's gone! He's gone!" And I knew that if she wasn't right, she was mighty close.

We called Mom and Dad's preacher, Ed Joice, to come, but Daddy kept hanging on. Then, once again, I knew in my heart that he would make it as he had dozens of times before. Everyone who knows him is quick to let you know that Bill Burden is tough.

But he is more than tough. He knows God, and he always

trusts his welfare to God's will. Surely he has fight. But he also keeps God in his corner, and he always talks to God "between rounds."

It was a beautiful day in the fall of 1969. Dad and Mother were on vacation in Weslaco, Texas, and Dad was doing what he loved to do most of all—fishing! He had only recently retired after thirty-seven years of working on oil leases and selling, part-time, fire extinguishers, fire hoses, and fire trucks, and now he and Mother were on a vacation, preparing to enjoy a life of retirement that they had most assuredly earned.

Suddenly, the vacation became a nightmare, a bad dream that waking up from could not end. Dad became ill. So ill, in fact, that hospitalization was required. After a week or so in the Weslaco hospital, he was transferred by his doctors to the famed Scott and White Memorial Hospital and Clinic in Temple, Texas. After extensive tests, clinic physicians announced their heartstopping diagnosis.

Dad had multiple myeloma—myeloma and plasmacytoma!

Myeloma is a great increase in the number of abnormal plasma cells found especially in the bone marrow. These cells destroy normal bone tissue and cause pain. In some cases victims suffer anemia; others have an increased susceptibility to infection.

Plasmacytoma is a mass of cancerous plasma cells in the bone.

In other words, Dad's body could no longer manufacture the blood necessary to keep him alive. Also, the myeloma meant that his bones would become weak and brittle.

As if this weren't bad enough, Dad already suffered from a problem known as hereditary hemorrhagic telangiectasia, a condition in which blemish-like marks appear either internally or externally on the body. These spots can, without warning, begin bleeding profusely. Dad has these marks throughout his body, inside and out. Dad's father had them, and the precedent was not good. Grandfather literally bled to death. Dad, bleeding internally and externally from the nose, was doing the same thing.

Before, his body was able to produce enough blood to counteract the loss of blood. But now that the myeloma and plasmacytoma had developed, blood transfusions were his only hope of staying alive.

The specialists at Scott and White told me that Dad would not live ninety days. At that time, he had already had more than thirty pints of blood.

They told me that the transfusions, so vital to his survival, would eventually become his enemy. His body would start rejecting the transfusions one day, and when this happened, death would not be far behind. And even if by some lucky chance his body accepted the blood, serum hepatitis would probably one day develop and take his life.

In a desperate attempt to check the problem, doctors at Scott and White used a drug called Alkeran, a mustard-type treatment that was supposed to destroy the myeloma cells. At that time, the treatment was very new. The critical factor was how much to administer: not enough and it would have no effect; too much and the patient became deathly ill. In one instance, Dad did become terribly sick from the medication, but he finally recovered from the reaction.

With the expert care of the physicians at Scott and White, Dad finally recovered enough to go home to die.

But even as he and Mother rode toward Kansas, neither knew that the episode in Texas was but the start of years of physical and mental anguish that would see Dad again and again approach the brink of death. Only a combination of miracles and a desire to stay alive kept him from going over that brink.

Fighting was nothing new to Dad. He had been forced to fight for survival most of his life. He and Mother were married in the midst of the Depression, and they lived in Oklahoma. I was born there during the Dust Bowl days when the dust was so thick that a person couldn't see the sun, and my parents had to put damp sheets over the top of the bed to keep from choking on the dust at night.

From Oklahoma, we moved to Kansas. Dad always managed to find work, enough so that his family wouldn't starve. He worked long, hard hours in the oil fields of southeastern Kansas, coming home so tired he often sat down on the front porch and fell asleep. In 1935 he started managing an oil lease and later, part-time, selling fire equipment, jobs he continued until his retirement in 1968.

But the fight he started in Texas was unlike any other he'd had before. Blood transfusions became his lifeline. There were days, indeed weeks, of pain and agony with Dad clinging to life by sheer courage and determination; feeling, believing, that if he just held on long enough, things would work out.

Time and again he would have to go to the hospital to receive the transfusions. At the writing of this book, he has set medical history by having received 335 pints of blood, averaging two pints every transfusion. One time he required eight pints of blood without a break in the transfusions.

During the ninety-seventh transfusion, it happened. His body started rejecting the foreign blood.

"You shake like a leaf in a windstorm," is how Dad describes the body rejecting a transfusion. The shaking is accompanied by chills and cramps.

But he hung on, and he survived that transfusion. Finally,

the doctor prescribed a medicine to counter the rejection problem.

Because of Dad's condition, his veins are generally fairly well collapsed, making it almost impossible to find a vein for the transfusion needle.

But Dad has categorically said, "You will never do a 'cut-down' on me!"

A cut-down occurs when the veins are so difficult to find that the doctor literally has to cut down into the wrist and pull up a vein in which to stick the needle, a very gruesome procedure.

I have seen the nurse stick the needle into Dad's wrist, between his fingers, into his ankles, and between his toes, trying to find a vein.

I have seen nurse after nurse, as white as a sheet, come out of Dad's room and get another nurse, telling her, "I can't stick that man one more time."

One time at the hospital in Coffeyville, Kansas, I saw six nurses, one at a time, "give up," and they finally got the doctor on duty to find a vein.

But do you know what Dad was doing the entire time?

With the tightest fist he could muster and the biggest smile he could get on his face, he'd say, each time, to the nurse, "Come on, you'll get it this time!"

This positive mental attitude on Dad's part, coupled with prayer, has kept him alive when all odds in the books have said he wouldn't last another day.

Through all the trials and tribulations these past ten years, Dad has never given up. He and Mother have logged thousands of miles getting to various doctors in various cities — from those at the Scott and White Clinic in Temple, Texas, to those at the Kansas University Medical Center in Kansas City; from those in Tulsa and Bartlesville, Oklahoma, to those in Wichita, Kansas, to those in Milwaukee, to those at the Cancer

Clinic in Colorado Springs; each time seeking a cure for the myeloma and plasmacytoma. But no one had a cure.

In fact, the doctors at the Cancer Clinic in Colorado Springs forecast an even gloomier future, saying that one day Dad would be eating something and his jaw would break, or he'd roll over in bed and his ribs would break, so brittle would the bones become.

The doctors have given Dad good news about as often as water ski tournaments are held at the North Pole. But Dad refuses to give up. He clings to life as tightly as morning dew hugs the flowers. Dad believes that God has a plan for him and it is through Him that Dad is alive today. Maybe now it's only to be a good example for others who find the going getting tough. But whatever it is, Dad is ready.

Dr. William K. Walker, Dad's personal physician, who has seen Dad through some very tough times, shakes his head in amazement when asked about Dad.

W. H. "Bill" Burden and Dr. William K. Walker

"He's tops in the area of toughness, of not complaining," Dr. Walker said.

Time and again Dr. Walker has walked into Dad's hospital room with a heavy heart, wondering if Dad would stay alive until the next day. Yet Dad always makes it easy for Dr. Walker to be open and honest.

Dad is one of that rare breed of people who, despite their own problems, is always concerned about the other fellow. He endeavors to make Dr. Walker and the nurses feel relaxed and comfortable when they're in his room.

He is generally more interested in talking with Dr. Walker about fishing than he is about his own condition.

Dad is living proof that a belief in God and in God's plan for an individual, and a positive outlook on life, can get one through the most terrible pain and agony.

The question arises today—does Dad still have myeloma and plasmacytoma or not?

Dr. Walker believes that given enough time, the human body can develop resistance to any sort of virus or disease, including cancer. He can't explain exactly how it happens, but the human body is a wonderful, complex piece of machinery, and he does believe that it can happen. And if this is so, there is a ray of hope, slender perhaps but there nonetheless, that anyone who contracts a catastrophic disease, if he can just get tough and hold out long enough, can conquer the disease.

But how does one hold out?

Dr. Walker gave me a list of characteristics people such as Dad seem to possess:

Faith in God
Faith in their doctors
Accepting the fact that they have a certain illness

Accepting the uncertainties of life and the hard knocks it can
  hand out
Never comparing their problems to those of others

Dad has often said, "Everyone has his own problems, and
he's got to either live with them or die with them, so the best
thing to do is to make the most of them."

Those who manage to hang on when the odds are over-
whelmingly against them share another common trait. Dr.
Walker told me, "They never quit; they are not defeatists."

It would be grossly unfair not to mention the role my mother
has played in keeping Dad alive all these years. Often the
spouse suffers as much anguish as, if not more than, the person
with the affliction. And he or she usually suffers in silence.

Many has been the night that Mother has rushed Dad to the
hospital in the middle of the night to get a desperately needed
transfusion. Many nights she has sat by his bedside from dusk
until dawn helping him in every way she could, ministering to
his needs or just giving him moral support. Too, many has been
the night that she has waited impatiently as the highway patrol
has rushed blood the 100 miles from Wichita in a frantic effort
to save Dad's life.

She has been tremendous through all of this. She has never
complained even when she showed evidence of total exhaus-
tion.

Mother credits her friends and fellow church members for
her continued strength. "Never underestimate what your
friends and church people can do for you when you're in these
spots," she says. "You can't put a value on friendship and your
church people because you just can't go through this world
alone."

So far the story about Dad has dwelt upon the fact that he has refused to give up, refused to lie down and die as he could have done on many occasions. Dad is tough, there's no question about that. But it would be remiss not to mention that he has had his weak moments, sometimes even periods of delusion. The important thing is that he has never wallowed in self-pity.

"I almost gave up once in the hospital," Dad recalls. "Then a friend visited me and gave me a new outlook on life. For over an hour he read the 'riot act' to me. He'd been through some tough times too. His wife had to give him mouth-to-mouth resuscitation once.

"He told me that I didn't have half the trouble others had. I made up my mind right then and there to live with my problems. Well, he came along just in the nick of time because he made me realize that there's always someone worse off than yourself."

But Dad's story is not over. He continues to live on the knife-edge between life and death. He still requires blood transfusions, but he refuses to give up. He faces each day as positively as he can. He is an inspiration to those around him. He simply doesn't quit.

In a couple of months, Dad and Mother will celebrate their fiftieth wedding anniversary. For the past ten years Dad has always kept his next goal, his next destination, uppermost in his mind.

Right now his goal is to live until their fiftieth wedding anniversary. He has told me that he wants to be around to hold in his hands a copy of this book. So after their fiftieth wedding anniversary, that will be his next goal. After that, he'll find yet another goal and still another. Each of us shares his goals in our prayers.

> All and things, whatsoever ye shall ask in prayer, believing, ye shall receive.
>
> Matthew 21:22

I know, Joyce knows, Mother knows, my brother, Bob, and his wife, Francis, know, the grandchildren know, and, yes, Dad knows that one day it will be God's will for Dad to cross over to that heavenly life beyond. And when the roll is called up yonder, I'm sure Dad will be there.

Tough? Sure! But he's more than just tough. At the writing of this book Dad is living proof that knowing God can keep one tough when all else fails.

I suppose that the greatest observation I have ever made about my Dad is that he always practices what he preaches.

When I was still a boy living at home, he told me once about a little sign that hung on the wall of the high school gymnasium where he went to school. And now that I've seen my Dad prove its worth, I hope I'll remember its words as long as I live.

The little sign simply read,

"When the Great Scorer comes to write against your name, He writes not that you won or lost, but how you played the game."

13
How Do the Tough
Get Tough?

Eight little words?
Yes, eight little words.

I AM. . . .
I SHOULD. . . .
I CAN. . . .
I WILL. . . .

I AM God's creation.
I AM a part of His plan.
I AM willing to accept the things I cannot change.

I SHOULD count my blessings.
I SHOULD turn my scars into stars.
I SHOULD change the things I can.

147

I CAN ask God for a miracle.

I CAN, with His help, turn my lemons into lemonade.

I CAN have faith and hope.

I WILL seek Divine guidance.

I WILL reach for the stars.

I WILL do my best.

Things turn out best for those who make the best of the way things turn out.

And those who make the best of the way things turn out are the ones who can honestly say to themselves, "I AM . . . I SHOULD . . . I CAN . . . and I WILL."

There are times in life when things happen over which we have no control. There are times in life when it is difficult and times when it is even impossible to understand why things happen the way they do. But one thing is certain. Those who are able to get tough when the going gets that way are the ones who are able to accept the things that they cannot change. They are the ones who are able to accept the fact that God has a reason for everything.

They do not wallow in self-pity. They trust God, and they know that He has a plan for their lives.

They analyze their situation. They count their blessings. They take a close look at their inner being.

From every adversity the seed of something good can grow.

But too often we let the pain of the moment cloud our thinking. Too often we cannot see beyond now.

In the span of a lifetime, we encounter many experiences: some good, some bad—but each one an experience just the same.

The question is—do we make the best of the way things turn out?

Glenn Cunningham said, "I AM badly burned. I SHOULD force my legs to move. I CAN walk again. I WILL even run again." And run he did. He ran the world's fastest mile.

Art Linkletter said "I AM without a daughter. I SHOULD overcome my anger. I CAN turn my scars into stars. I WILL help others through my experience." Traveling more than a quarter of a million miles each year, he has dedicated his energies to sharing facts about drug abuse with children and parents.

Marguerite Piazza said, "I AM faced with cancer. I SHOULD fight to live for my children's sake. I CAN whip this thing. I WILL sing again and rebuild my career." And rebuild her career she did. Four months after undergoing radical surgery, she sang at President Richard Nixon's inauguration. Now, even after cancer was discovered a second time, making seventy-two consecutive hours of radiation therapy necessary, she is singing again and living a happy life.

John and Greg Rice each said, "I AM smaller than normal. I SHOULD accept what I cannot change. I CAN think big. WE WILL be two dimes in a handful of nickels." Today, they travel all over the world giving hope to others with their story of what it is like to be little men in a big man's world. And they truly are two dimes of special mintage in a handful of nickels.

Dave Yoho said, "I AM unable to speak like everyone else. I SHOULD change my attitude about myself and about others. I CAN overcome my inner feelings of rejection and nonworth. I WILL become a rule maker instead of a rule breaker." He realized that his speech impediment was a gift from God, given to him in His wisdom because of some special plan He had in mind for him. Each year he trains thousands of salesmen, and his greatest thrill comes from helping others realize that they must accept themselves unconditionally if they are going to discover God's plan for their lives.

Carol Schuller said, "I AM missing a leg. I SHOULD look at what I have left. I CAN walk down the aisle at my sister's wedding. I WILL lead a normal life." And today she is an active teenager. Once again, she enjoys feeling the cold winter breezes on her face as she races down the side of a mountain on skis.

Ben B. Franklin said, "I AM paralyzed from the waist down. I SHOULD accept God's will. I CAN get around without a wheelchair. I WILL move about with the use of crutches, leg braces, and a back brace." And move about he did—through the Amazon jungle in a dugout canoe, across the desert on the back of a camel, through the Colorado high country on a horse—visiting one hundred and twelve foreign countries, and nearly every exotic locale known to man.

Earl Nightingale said, "I AM curious why so many are in such bad financial shape. I SHOULD find the answers. I CAN prepare myself so that I will be ready for opportunity when I meet it. I WILL stay with it." And stay with it he did. Today, his daily radio program, "Our Changing world," is carried on more than one thousand radio stations, and an estimated thirty million people tune in each day to hear what he has to say.

Mary Crowley said, "I AM responsible for the welfare of my two children. I SHOULD go to work. I CAN solve my problems. I WILL trust in the Lord." And God watched out for her. Through the years her faith in the Lord and her perseverance have paid off. Today, Home Interiors and Gifts, Inc. is a multimillion-dollar company and sells millions of dollars worth of merchandise each year and numbers associates of over 30,000 people, mostly housewives.

Charlie Plumb said, "I AM a prisoner of war. I SHOULD maintain my faith in God and in my country. I CAN endure whatever comes. I WILL survive." For six years he was able to endure beatings, physical and mental torture, humiliation, and deprivation in a man-made hell on earth. Even while suffering the lowliest existence a man could have, he kept his faith in God, and he was able to survive.

W. H. "Bill" Burden said, "I AM facing a tough fight with multiple myeloma and plasmacytoma. I SHOULD accept the uncertainties ahead. I CAN live with my problems. I WILL be proud of what the Great Scorer writes against my name."

As the final chapter of this book was being written, I got a phone call early one morning from Mother telling me that Dad had gone to be with the Lord.

He did not live to celebrate their fiftieth wedding anniversary, but the fact that he had that as his goal made the end a little more peaceful. He stayed tough right to the end.

The faith and the hope that had sustained him for so many years continued to sustain him during his last hours on this earth.

He and Mother spent his last day together before she left to go home for the night. He appeared fine. He ate a good evening meal. At 10:30 that evening, he drank all of his orange juice. At midnight he drank his glass of medicine. Forty-five minutes later, when the nurse went to his bed to check on him, he was fine, but as she turned to leave the room, he made a little sound and then, just as quickly, he was gone.

Dad knew that one day the Great Scorer would come to write against his name, and he wanted Him to be able to write, "Here is a great example. Even though things were tough for him, he did his best."

It was at a Positive Thinking Rally in Tulsa, Oklahoma, May 15, 1979. I had just finished speaking and was at the autograph booth during the intermission when a lady walked up to me with tears in her eyes. In February, the doctors had discovered that she had cancer. Since then her life had been a trial, a difficult contest, and she was losing.

"Now that I've heard the story of your father, I think I can make it," she said.

Before that day, she had mentally given up. Life meant nothing to her. She was defeated. Her morale, her spirit, was at rock bottom. But now, she had a spark of life again, a spark of hope and determination. The doctors might say that she had cancer, but if someone else could keep on keeping on, so could she.

I have shared Dad's story with countless audiences and invariably somewhere in each audience there had been someone, like the lady in Tulsa, who needed a ray of hope. Or like the young man in Memphis who, three days before, had unsuccessfully tried to end it all.

Maybe Dad stayed tough because he felt that God wanted me to share his story with others. Certainly, I will continue to tell his story because I believe that he proved that prayer and positive thinking and eight little words can make the difference.

So it is with this book. If a close look at the lives of those in this book can help just one person who has not yet found the eight little words, then it will have been worth all of the effort it took to write it.

I've been a positive thinker all of my life, and in 1962 I wrote a poem entitled, "As a Man Thinketh." Through the years, as I have studied the lives of men and women and boys and girls who were able to get tough when the going got that way, this poem has taken on added meaning for me. I hope it will bring inspiration to you.

As a Man Thinketh

I felt disheartened, dead with despair;
Problems were mine everywhere.
Nothing seemed to go quite right,
So I lived with hate and spite.

Then one day I looked upward to the sky,
And I lifted my thoughts just as high.
Unchained at last was my soul.
So I marched onward toward my goal.

Good fortune now has come my way,
And I know in my heart it's here to stay.
Because I've found life's magic key,
AS A MAN THINKETH, SO HE SHALL BE.

If you would like to have a complimentary copy of "As a Man Thinketh," printed on 8" x 10" parchtex for framing, I would be happy to send one to you. You may write me at P. O. Box 5500, Lakeland, Florida 33803.

In the way of an epitaph to my life on this earth, I hope they'll put eight little words on my tomb.

"I AM . . . I SHOULD . . . I CAN . . . I WILL. . . ."

Finally, in addition to these eight little words, I can tell you that there are two more words that serve as the "frosting on the cake."

These two little words can be spoken only by those who have found and used the other eight words.

And these two little words are so rewarding. They are the words—"I DID."

I pray that you will always remember the eight little words. If you do, then I know that you will be able to get tough when the going gets that way!

God bless you.

Billy Bruder